BUILDING PROSPERITY

Financing Public Infrastructure for Economic Development

P9-APB-723

GOVERNMENT FINANCE RESEARCH CENTER
of the
MUNICIPAL FINANCE OFFICERS ASSOCIATION

Government Finance Research Center
Municipal Finance Officers Association

This technical assistance study was prepared by the Government Finance Research Center of the Municipal Finance Officers Association under contract with the Economic Development Administration. The findings, conclusions, recommendations, and other statements in this report are solely those of the contractor and do not necessarily reflect the views of the Municipal Finance Officers Association or the Economic Development Administration.

Building Prosperity: Financing Public Infrastructure for Economic Development is published through a grant from the Economic Development Administration of the U.S. Department of Commerce. No parts may be reproduced without permission from the Economic Development Administration and the Government Finance Research Center of the Municipal Finance Officers Association.

Library of Congress catalog card number: 83-62941
ISBN: 0-89125-079-4

October 1983
.Second printing, March 1985

Government Finance Research Center
1750 K Street, NW, Suite 200
Washington, DC 20006
202/466-2014

TABLE OF CONTENTS

FOREWORD

The MFOA Bylaws state that a general goal of the Association is "to develop, improve, and publish a body of knowledge in governmental finance management." An important component of that knowledge is a better understanding of how the public infrastructure and its financing affect not only governmental finances, but contribute to the overall economic health—the prosperity—of communities, states, and the nation. General financial management in government is, after all, only a subset of the larger question of efficiently and responsibly managing the nation's overall resources—public and private.

As is noted in the Preface, this volume is the product of many contributors, as assembled in research conducted by the MFOA's Government Finance Research Center, jointly funded by the MFOA and the Economic Development Administration of the U.S. Department of Commerce. To the many involved in its preparation, I extend my personal appreciation.

Jeffrey L. Esser
Executive Director
Municipal Finance Officers
Association

PREFACE

This volume represents the first of several studies done by the Government Finance Research Center of the Municipal Finance Officers Association (MFOA) relating to the financing of public infrastructure and its role in economic development. Its intent is to survey the irregular and complicated landscape of the needs for and financing of public works in this country, especially focusing on the role of state and local governments.

In developing the analysis, we have attempted to separate rhetoric from analysis and assertion from fact and present an objective assessment of where states and localities are heading—or might go—in their increasingly difficult quest for capital financing. Readers will, we hope, come away with a better notion of the size of capital financing tasks that lie ahead and what are the more realistic alternatives that are at hand in meeting those financing needs. As we point out in the following pages, the current difficulties and cutbacks in financing public works are endemic to the changing times and the reconsideration of many of the traditional roles and responsibilities of government at all levels. Amid the turbulence of change, new ideas are constantly emerging, and many of them may succeed where old methods are no longer useful or feasible. In any event, the struggle for capital resources, especially those that are to be committed for many years in the provision of public services, will continue to make heavy demands on the creativity and courage of public officials.

Acknowledgements

As infrastructure is a construct of many parts, many persons have contributed to the concept and the realization of this volume: Government Finance Research Center staff, members of the Advisory Committee to this project, colleagues from state and local professional and interest groups, and technical advisors from the U.S. Economic Development Administration.

Research and authorship are the work of Government Finance Research Center members Michael P. Buckley, Lisa A. Cole, Jeffrey Davison, Patricia M. Hawkins, Wesley C. Hough, Amy L. Reimann, Barbara Weiss, and Paul Zorn. The Project Manager was Barbara Weiss, and as Director of the GFRC, I provided overall guidance as the Project Director. Production support was the province of Allison McLuckie, Jill Wakefield, and Patricia Williams.

The contributions of members of the Advisory Committee lent valuable insights from a wide range of experience in both the public service and the private sector. Their assistance is gratefully acknowledged.

The assistance of Catherine L. Spain, Director of the Federal Liaison Center of the Municipal Finance Officers Association, was a beacon through the fog of federal legislation.

Maintaining a focus on the needs of local officials for technical assistance was the role of George Gould, Felicity Gillette, and Leon Douglas of the Office of Planning, Technical Assistance, Research and Evaluation of the U.S. Economic Development Administration.

A special thanks is extended to the Public Securities Association for permission to use its art work on the cover of this book. Publication direction was given by Ms. Rebecca Russum, Municipal Finance Officers Association, and typesetting was done by Harper Graphics, Inc.

John E. Petersen
Director, Government Finance
Research Center

FINANCING INFRASTRUCTURE FOR ECONOMIC DEVELOPMENT
RESEARCH PROJECT ADVISORY COMMITTEE

Jeff Apfel,
New York State Development and Planning,
Governor's Office.

Donald W. Beatty,
Vice President,
Alliance Capital Management Corporation.

Bernard Berkowitz,
President,
Baltimore Economic Development Corporation.

Russell Blake,
City Manager,
Pocomoke City, Maryland.

Sandra Brewer,
City Councilwoman,
Hinesville, Georgia.

Douglas E. Carter,
Finance Director,
City of Charlotte, North Carolina.

James Dausch,
Senior Vice President,
The Rouse Company.

Robert Doty,
Partner,
Squire, Sanders & Dempsey.

Betty Diener,
Secretary, Commerce and Resources,
Commonwealth of Virginia.

Eugene Franchett,
Executive Director,
Metropolitan Council of the Twin Cities Area.

Alan J. Karcher,
Speaker,
New Jersey General Assembly.

James L. Martin,
Public Works Director,
City of Fresno, California.

Melvin A. Mister,
Vice President, Money Market Division,
Citibank.

Charles T. Noona,
Senior Vice President,
Municipal Research Department,
L.F. Rothschild, Unterberg, Towbin.

Pamela Plumb,
City Counselor,
City of Portland, Maine.

Lawrence Shubnell,
Vice President,
Government Finance Associates.

James Young,
Executive Vice President,
Finance and Administration,
Cabot Cabot & Forbes.

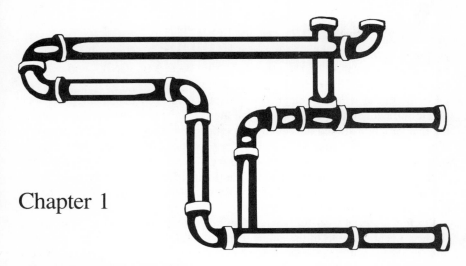

Chapter 1

THE INFRASTRUCTURE CONNECTION

Streets and sidewalks collapse in the wake of a sewer line explosion in Louisville, Kentucky. An interstate bridge in Connecticut breaks, plunging trucks and vacationers 75 feet into the Mianus River. A broken water main under New York's garment district floods key electrical connections and renders the central section of the nation's largest city without power for days. A sampling of the headlines is enough to glimpse the anger, and sometimes fear, aroused in the public as the nation's public facilities—the infrastructure—wear out and fall apart. An exhaustive list of recent infrastructure failures throughout the nation could fill the pages of a volume this size.

But, breakdowns and blackouts are not at the center of attention in this work. Rather, what can be done to avoid them, or correct them when they occur, is the major concern. The engineering and technology, while surely subject to improvement, have largely been mastered and do not in themselves act as the major constraint on doing something to correct the situation. It is not so much a question of knowing what to do as having the means, the wherewithal, with which to do it. Obtaining the means, in this case, is a matter of money. Money—collected through taxes, fees, or public borrowing or through private assumption of responsibilities—is the adhesive that makes the infrastructure take shape and, subsequently, hang together. So, this book is about building infrastructure—airports, bridges, waterworks, and sewers, to name a few—but in the special sense of how they are financed.

We care about infrastructure and its financing because public works are vital not only to domestic peace and tranquility but also to the nation's prosperity. In this country, the basic sinews of the transportation network and the use, production, and control of the water resources are operated and financed by the

1

public sector. Furthermore, the capital facilities used in public schools, hospitals, jails, and governmental buildings of all descriptions contribute to the productivity, health, and safety of the nation's private sector, its goods, workers, and capital stock.

At the outset it is important to note that the lines of demarcation between public infrastructure and private capital are not sharply drawn, and are subject to great variation around the country. In some parts of the land, public provision of power facilities, health care, and higher education is very much the tradition. In others, such activities are a private endeavor (although usually much aided or regulated by governmental entities). Furthermore, even within the government sector, what is the province of local government in one major region may be that of the state government in another.

Placing price tags on the value of infrastructure and deciding who should finance it is at the heart of the political process. While great variation is evident, none can deny that the prosperity of us all is tightly intertwined with the physical adequacy and fiscal viability of the nation's publicly-owned capital stock.

A Concert of Connections

When one conjures up thoughts of infrastructure, it most likely is an image of various walls, pipes, and paving—a mosaic of planes and angles, tubes and sockets, bricks and mortar—that ultimately fit together for the provision of needed services. And so it is with the financial underpinnings of the infrastructure. By its technological nature, infrastructure typically involves large sums of money committed for long periods to the intended benefit of a diverse number of users that most likely will change over time. As the benefits are to be enjoyed by many through the passage of considerable time and across wide areas in a frequently complex pattern, so the financing arrangements themselves often reflect the many and varied connections among the planners, builders, and benefiters.

Thus, to discuss the financing of infrastructure is to discuss many connections between public infrastructure and private prosperity, between revenue bases and the ability to finance public infrastructure, between a government's capital budget and its operating expenditures, between federal aid programs and state and local capital financing.

This volume will attempt to give the "big picture" as a composite of the many little pictures that make up that larger and complicated composite of the infrastructure problem and its many and diverse solutions. Most of the focus will be on state and local governments since these units are the major direct providers of public infrastructure.

Condition of Public Facilities

America's infrastructure is in trouble. Despite earlier public investments of hundreds of billions of dollars, the nation's public capital assets are now suffering from years of neglect, overuse, deferred maintenance, and delayed repairs. Rehabilitation and new construction have been curtailed. This practice of "disinvestment" in basic public facilities is widespread, both in terms of the types of physical structures and their locations. It has occurred not only in the older, declining and fiscally troubled cities such as Cleveland, Boston, and New York, but in suburban and rural communities in every region of the country. It is evident not only among such highly visible structures as highways and bridges, but also concealed in jails, dams, sewers, and water supply systems that frequently escape public view.

A pivotal factor accounting for this situation has been the 15-year decline in the amount of spending for capital purposes by all levels of government. Since 1965, federal, state, and local governments have reduced their investments in public facilities, in real dollar terms, by almost 30 percent. Public works investment by all levels of government shrank from 4.1 percent of the Gross National Product in 1965 to less than 1.5 percent in 1982.

The condition of deteriorating infrastructure and inadequate financing of public facilities moved to the forefront of national attention and interest in recent years, becoming the subject of intense discussion by the media, government and trade associations, citizens' groups, and the Congress. Research documenting the public works decline has been picked up by the popular press and embellished with a growing litany of crumbling highways, rusty bridges, leaking water systems, unsafe dams, obsolete port facilities, aging public buildings, and overcrowded prisons.[1] Estimates of the enormous costs of rebuilding the nation's public works have varied widely, and the list of obstacles that all levels of government face in addressing this issue is a long one.

What is the condition of the nation's capital stock? How much will it cost to repair? A response to these two questions is not a simple task, but many are hard at the answers. There never have been a nationwide inventory and assessment of the country's public works, and there are no national standards for analyzing the need to repair or replace public facilities.

The following summary of some of the more serious infrastructure deficiencies by major category draws its information from research studies, government reports, and Congressional hearings.

Water

- The City of New York loses an average of 100 million gallons of water per day due to leaks in old water mains, 6,000 miles of which are at least 75 years old. Approximately 40 percent of Boston's purchased water is unaccounted for due to undermetering, pipeline leaks, breaks, and unmetered public uses. The Urban Institute, in a survey of 28 major cities, found that over one-third were losing 10 percent or more of their water because of deteriorating pipes.[2]
- Choate and Walter estimate in *America in Ruins* that the 756 urban areas with populations over 50,000 will have to spend between $75 billion and

$110 billion to maintain their urban water systems over the next two decades.[3]

- The old "Dustbowl" region of the U.S., which now accounts for 23 percent of the nation's irrigated farmland and produces 40 percent of its processed beef, is in danger of depleting its water resources. Under present conditions, it will be gone by the year 2000.[4]

Sewers

- About one-half of the nation's communities have wastewater treatment systems that are operating at full capacity and cannot support further industrial or residential growth. A 1978 survey found 46 percent of the 6,870 communities contacted were operating their treatment systems at 80 percent or more of their capacity.[5]
- To meet existing water pollution control standards, more than $31 billion will have to be invested in sewer systems and wastewater treatment plants over the next five years.[6]
- According to the 1982 *Needs Survey* conducted by EPA, there are $118.4 billion in wastewater treatment needs to serve the population to the year 2000.[7]

Highways

- The Federal Highway Administration predicts that nearly one-half of the 42,500 mile interstate highway system, if not repaired soon, will have to be replaced. The system requires replacement at a rate of 2,000 miles per year. Some 8,000 miles of the system are beyond their design service life and will have to be replaced. More than $33 billion worth of repairs will be required over the next decade.[8]
- The nation's other road systems are in even worse shape. According to estimates by the U.S. Department of Transportation (DOT), more than $500 billion will be needed over the next 10 years to maintain existing levels of service on non-urban highways.[9]
- The DOT estimated in 1980 that $315.2 billion in capital investment during the period of 1980–1995 would be needed to remove all highway deficiencies.[10]

Bridges

- Almost one-half of the nation's 557,516 bridges are considered by the Federal Highway Administration to be structurally deficient or functionally obsolete. More than 200,000 of today's bridges are more than 40 years old. Federal estimates of needed repairs total $47.6 billion. A review of past funding levels shows a replacement or repair rate of 866 bridges annually.[11]

Mass Transit

- Twenty percent of all subway cars are more than 25 years old, while their design life is estimated to be only 10 years. According to DOT, 67 percent of all mass transit track should be upgraded.[12]
- Between 1977 and 1981, the number of serious breakdowns recorded on New York's subway system tripled from 12,997 to 36,000. The number of miles traveled by a subway car before major repairs decreased from 13,627 in 1977 to 6,500 in 1981.[13]
- The American Public Transit Association estimates that $36.6 billion in capital improvements for mass transit are needed over the next 10 years.[14]

Jails

- As reported in *Business Week* magazine, over one-half of the nation's 3,500 correctional facilities are more than 30 years old. As many as 3,000 of them must either be rebuilt, expanded, or substantially rehabilitated over the next 10 years. Much of this repair work is mandated by the courts. The costs of such repair are estimated at over $8 billion.[15]

Estimating the Costs of Repair

Estimating the costs of fixing up the nation's public works has become almost a cottage industry as a wide variety of estimates have been developed. The Morgan Guaranty Trust Company of New York places the costs of repairing the nation's infrastructure at $500 billion by 1985.[16] The Associated General Contractors of America estimates total public construction needs of $909.9 billion.[17] Pat Choate, coauthor of *America in Ruins*, has estimated that $2.5 trillion to $3 trillion in public works investment is needed by 1995 just to maintain existing levels of services.[18] And the Urban Institute estimated that, due to neglect of the existing infrastructure, maintenance costs alone will shoot up to $860 billion over the next 15 years.[19]

The wide range of estimates is not without its critics, including many of the "estimators." All of the cost estimates use a variety of sources that have been developed in an *ad hoc* way. Some estimates are criticized as nothing more than wish lists; most greatly exceed the forecasts of future public spending for capital purposes. In Choate's words, "Whether it's $3 trillion or $103 trillion, we don't have the money."[20]

A study undertaken by the Congressional Budget Office (CBO) at the request of the Senate Committee on the Budget and published in April 1983 assessed the needs of seven infrastructure systems and the costs of meeting those needs. CBO concluded:

> Like estimates of the extent and severity of the nation's infrastructure problems, estimates of the costs of correcting those problems are necessarily

imprecise. To some extent, this reflects a lack of aggregate data and differences about what the definition of infrastructure includes. Overestimates may at times reflect the interests of affected parties. In addition, the orientation of current programs toward new construction tends to lead to overstated estimates of need. But most important, the costs of remedying these problems depend on the extent and quality of the infrastructure services the nation wishes to purchase. As a result of these uncertainties, estimates of the costs of meeting the nation's infrastructure needs range widely.[21]

Table 1 presents CBO's calculation of the amount of annual spending by governments (federal, state, and local) necessary to meet needs through 1990 under current federal policies for each of the seven major infrastructure systems. For the eight years in consideration (1983 to 1990), this amounts to $427 billion in capital outlays.

TABLE 1
Estimated Annual Capital Needs for Selected Infrastructure Programs Under Current Policy, 1983–1990
(In billions of 1982 dollars)

Infrastructure System	Annual Capital Spending			Effective Federal Share of Total
	Total	New Construction	Repair, Rehabilitiation, and Replacement	
Highways	27.2	9.9	17.3	13.1
Public Transit	5.5	2.2	3.3	4.1
Wastewater Treatment	6.6	6.1	0.5	4.2
Water Resources	4.1	2.3	1.8	3.7
Air Traffic Control	0.8	0.1	0.7	0.8
Airports	1.5	1.0	0.5	0.9
Municipal Water Supply	7.7	3.6	4.1	1.4
Total	53.4	25.2	28.2	28.2

SOURCE: Congressional Budget Office.

A discussion of the costs of repairing the nation's capital stock cannot overlook the indirect, but no less considerable, costs of infrastructure neglect. While such costs are difficult to calculate, inadequate public facilities impose substantial burdens on the economy in terms of delays, increased wear and tear on equipment, and reduced productivity. The costs of impeded transportation immediately come to mind. For example, one study found that a road in poor condition may lead to operating costs for motor vehicles that are 15 to 29 percent higher than costs on a road in good condition.[22] When an aging water main breaks, thousands of people and numerous businesses are affected. Polluted water supplies threaten public health. The lack of adequate capacity of water and sewer facilities can prevent existing industries from expanding and hamper residential development.

There is now greater recognition of the connection between the decline of the country's public capital assets and current problems of economic development, growth, and employment. It has been estimated that between half and three-fourths of the nation's communities will be unable to participate in future economic recovery until major new investments are made in their basic facilities.[23] Unfortunately, the demand for renewed public capital investment occurs at a time when the resources to finance it are flagging: "all revenues are combining with an inability to borrow in a way that is making it extremely difficult for federal, state, and local governments to fulfill their traditional role of providing the public infrastructure facilities needed for economic expansion and development."[24]

Infrastructure Spending Trends

A review of government spending patterns makes clear that underinvestment in maintenance, rehabilitation, and replacement of public facilities over a long period of time underlies the present situation. The most comprehensive nationwide data on public works investment are found in the research and reports of the CONSAD Research Corporation undertaken with the sponsorship of the U.S. Department of Commerce and published in 1980. CONSAD data show that total investment in public works by federal, state, and local governments, measured in constant 1972 dollars, reached a peak in 1968. Measured in noninflated purchasing power, the nation's public capital investments fell from $33.7 billion in 1965 to less than $24 billion in 1980, a 30 percent decline.[25]

State and local governments account for a large portion of the decline, as illustrated in Table 2. Since 1968, state and local capital investment has fallen 37 percent, from a high of $35.9 billion to $22.3 billion (in constant 1972 dollars) in 1982.[26] Measured in per capita terms, state and local public works investment declined from $179 per person in 1968 to $96 per person 14 years later. Capital expenditures make up a smaller share of total outlays of state and local governments: in 1960, state and local governments spent 25 percent of their budgets on infrastructure; by 1982 they were spending only 14 percent.

At the federal level, the creation of numerous social programs during the 1960s shifted the federal government's attention away from capital spending programs. As federal budget priorities shifted to meet current services and transfer payment needs, grants to states and localities—while nominally growing—failed to keep pace with the explosive growth in grants for operating purposes.[27] Whereas in the mid 1960s, 44 percent of total federal aid to state and local governments went for public works, by 1980, this figure had dropped to only 25 percent. The magnitude of this trend takes on more significance in the context of state and local governments' increasing dependence on federal aid for public improvements. Federal assistance now accounts for approximately 40 percent of all state and local capital outlays, up from its 10 percent share in 1957.[28]

This slowdown in capital spending, and the resulting massive disinvestment in the public capital stock, has been laid at the doorstep of budget balancing,

TABLE 2
Capital Investment by States and Local Governments

| | Millions of Dollars | | Per Capita | |
Year	Current Dollars	Constant (1972) Dollars	Current Dollars	Constant (1972) Dollars
1968	26,898	35,896	134.02	178.85
1969	27,357	34,016	134.98	167.83
1970	27,773	31,844	135.56	155.43
1971	29,153	30,867	140.39	148.64
1972	30,247	30,483	144.10	145.23
1973	32,824	30,789	154.90	145.29
1974	39,939	31,840	186.76	148.89
1975	41,326	30,078	191.35	139.27
1976	39,354	27,947	180.49	128.18
1977	38,336	25,710	174.07	116.74
1978	45,753	27,642	205.55	124.19
1979	48,428	25,337	215.18	112.58
1980	53,825	25,326	236.38	111.22
1981	52,287	23,328	227.48	101.49
1982	50,956	22,258	219.58	95.92

SOURCE: U.S. General Accounting Office and Bureau of Economic Analysis.

holding down the rate of tax growth, and financing a growing menu of social services.[29] Some of the decline in public works spending can be attributed to decreases in capital outlays for highways as the interstate highway system nears completion, as well as to a slowdown in school construction as school-age population declines. Also, the assumption by the private sector of a greater role in the construction of public facilities can account for some.

The pattern of reallocating government expenditures to meet the increased demands for services and social programs has been confirmed in field research conducted by the Urban Institute, the U.S. Department of Commerce, the General Accounting Office, and others.[30] For example, in 1976, the City of New York, suffering from a severe fiscal crisis, cut its capital budget in half. During the same year, Buffalo reduced its spending for public improvements by one-third, while Pittsburgh cut its capital budget by 20 percent. The City of Cleveland increased total expenditures by 162 percent from 1972–1977; however, during the same period, capital spending increased only 37 percent.

Surveys of Current Practices

A survey of cities conducted in December 1982, by the National League of Cities (NLC) and the U.S. Conference of Mayors (USCM) developed an extensive data bank from more than 800 cities responding to questions concerning the physical condition of capital facilities. The cities also reported their ability to finance the repair, rehabilitiation, and replacement of capital facilities and their capital budgeting practices. The organizations jointly published an initial assessment of the survey data in April 1983.

The NLC-USCM data show that the cost of meeting high priority public facility needs in the cities is relatively modest, while the cities' abilities to finance their needs vary widely by region, population size, and city type. The findings also document the belief that economic development plays a significant role in local capital planning and budgeting: the cities, reporting the reasons they use for choosing priorities for public works facilities, ranked economic development as their third most important consideration, ranking it very close in priority with (1) the protection of public health and safety, and (2) the provision of essential services.[31]

The survey questionnaire asked city officials about 19 types of capital facilities. More than half of the respondents judged their community social service facilities, parks and recreational facilities, water storage, public building, water treatment, and traffic control equipment facilities to be in good condition. The facilities cited most frequently in need of major repair, rehabilitation, or replacement by 50 percent of the cities were streets and roads, sidewalks and curbs, and storm-water and sewage collection.

Survey respondents ranked the facilities according to their city's ability to bear the costs of maintenance, repair, and replacement. A majority of cities indicated that they could finance necessary work for public buildings, sidewalks and curbs, water distribution, water storage, and traffic control equipment out of their own resources. But, approximately one-third or more said that they required some degree of state or federal aid to finance the necessary work for streets and roads, bridges, wastewater treatment, parks and recreational facilities, stormwater collection and drainage, and sewage collection.

When assessing the city needs and potentials, it is important to note that traditional spending patterns play an important part in what the cities believe they can and cannot afford. For example, streets and roads, wastewater treatment, and parks and recreation have been the objects of large and important federal aid programs in the past. Water supply, curbs and gutters, and traffic control have typically relied on local sources for the bulk of their funding.

The National League of Cities-U.S. Conference of Mayors' initial assessment of the survey data concludes that the significant differences among respondents in terms of priorities and in condition of specific types of public facilities suggests that any national effort in this area should rely primarily on local planning and local priorities.

A survey conducted by the Government Finance Research Center for the Joint Economic Committee (JEC) queried over 300 cities on their fiscal year 1982 budgets and 1981 fiscal performance. Two out of every five cities in the survey reported that current operating outlays and debt service payments exceeded current revenues and receipts in 1981, with 59 percent projecting deficits in 1982.[32] Despite the heavy publicity surrounding the issue of capital investment, cities in 1981 realized only 60 percent of the spending they had budgeted for capital projects.

At the state level, many state governments are reporting record revenue short-falls despite increases in state sales and income taxes. Crisis management and program cutbacks are becoming standard operating procedures in many state capitols. The fiscal condition of the states, which is surveyed annually by the National Governors' Association, was reported in June 1983, to be at its lowest point since the Great Depression. Forty-seven states adopted budget balancing measures in fiscal 1983; prominent among them were hiring limits implemented in 42 states, selective program cuts put into effect by 37 states, and temporary or permanent revenue increases enacted in 33 states.[33]

Current fiscal conditions dictate that state and local governments look beyond traditional financing approaches to meet their needs for increased capital spending. The municipal securities market, a key capital financing source for state and local governments, is in a period of turbulent change, plagued by high interest costs, wide fluctuations in bond prices, and increased competition from new tax-exempt instruments and tax-shelter devices. Many state and local governments have already begun to respond with a variety of nontraditional approaches, such as setting up independent authorities to operate public facilities, increasing the application of user fees and charges, contracting out the delivery of public services to the private sector, and using creative financing techniques to raise capital for public improvements.

The complexity and scope of the nation's crumbling public facilities can be seen as both a crisis and an opportunity. The crisis has been well documented. The challenge lies in seizing the opportunity "to revitalize the national delivery of the vital services . . . citizens demand and to put them on a sounder financial base."[34] Key challenges facing state and local governments are the identification and establishment of priorities for their infrastructure needs, and the development and application of a proper mix of financing methods to foster economic development while fairly allocating the costs of needed public improvements.

Summary

A vast assortment of factors has contributed to the deterioration of the nation's infrastructure. Construction delays, fraud and waste, fragmented decisionmaking, inflation, high interest costs, reduced access to credit markets, tax and expenditure limitations, voter rejection of bond issues, federal tax reforms, population changes—these and more have all played a part in the decline. Some of them will be examined in subsequent chapters of this book, but an exploration of the role of all of them is beyond the scope and purposes of this volume.

This introduction has presented an overview of America's infrastructure problem: the declining condition of the country's public facilities and the insufficient financing of the same. In recent months, the problem has been the subject of discussion by the media, government officials, business leaders, and the public. A review of current research reports and government studies reveals widespread deterioration and disrepair in all functional categories of public works. Estimates of the costs of repair vary widely, some running into the hundreds of billions of dollars. The central causative factor has been large-scale reductions in capital spending by all levels of governments. After accounting for inflation, public works investment has been cut nearly in half from its highwater mark of 1968. Prolonged inflation, volatile and uncertain capital markets, corruption and waste in public construction projects, and government delays have also contributed to the neglect and underfunding of the nation's capital assets.

There is a growing awareness that in mid 1983 defective or inadequate public facilities are the key obstacles to economic recovery in many parts of the country. The added costs of delays, increased repairs, and reduced productivity are limiting the opportunities for industrial and commercial expansion, resulting in the loss of jobs and deteriorating tax bases. However, due to severe fiscal constraints, most governments are unable to increase spending for public infrastructure through greater reliance on traditional capital financing methods. In the midst of looming budget deficits and shifts in spending priorities toward meeting the funding needs of social security, medicare, and defense, the federal government is expected to continue to reduce intergovernmental aid for capital purposes. The recent and projected cuts occur at a time when the states and localities are experiencing severe financing problems of their own.

The desultory performance of state and local government finances underscores the need to examine both conventional and innovative arrangements for financing the nation's public works. Traditional approaches need to be reviewed and revised, where necessary, to make the best use of limited public resources. Creative financing methods can be utilized, where appropriate, to tap new sources of revenues and increase the flexibility of state and local governments in public facilities financing.

The remainder of this book is organized into five chapters. Chapter two presents an overview of processes used by state and local governments in selecting capital financing alternatives. Chapter three surveys the array of alternatives available to cities, counties, and states for financing infrastructure improvements. Both traditional and creative techniques for raising capital are described. The fourth chapter discusses the intergovernmental dimension—federal and state roles in infrastructure financing. It focuses on recent and proposed changes in federal programs and policies affecting public infrastructure investment and summarizes the impacts of state policies on local infrastructure financing and economic development. The final chapter returns to the central theme—defining the connections between infrastructure and economic development—taking account of the many facets and levels of intergovernmental and private sector involvement. It looks to the future with a firm conviction that the governmental policies and initiatives of cities, towns, and counties across the nation must provide the bedrock upon which to lay the foundation for building prosperity.

Endnotes

[1]See *Time* magazine, April 27, 1981, "The Crumbling of America;" *Business Week*, October 18, 1981, "The Decay That Threatens Economic Growth;" *Newsweek* magazine,

August 2, 1982, "The Decaying of America;" and *The Washington Post*, November 21–23, 1982, "Roadblocks, Parts 1–4."

[2]*New York Times*, September 11, 1981, "Public Facilities Held Facing Crisis."

[3]Pat Choate and Susan Walter, *America in Ruins: Beyond the Public Works Pork Barrel*, (Washington, DC: Council of State Planning Agencies), 1981, p. 2 (hereafter cited as Choate and Walter, *Ruins*).

[4]Pat Choate, "House Wednesday Group Special Report on U.S. Economic Infrastructure," (Washington, DC: House Wednesday Group), 1982, p. 1 (hereafter cited as Choate, "Wednesday").

[5]Associated General Contractors of America, *Our Fractured Framework: Why America Must Rebuild*, (Washington, DC: Associated General Contractors of America), 1982, p. 17.

[6]Choate and Walter, *Ruins*, p. 10.

[7]Clint Page, "$118 Billion by Year 2000 for Sewers," *Nation's Cities Weekly*, January 10, 1983, p. 1.

[8]William F. Clinger, Jr., "Testimony before the Task Force on the Budget Process, House Rules Committee," (Washington, DC: mimeo), September 15, 1982, p. 1.

[9]Melinda Beck et al., "The Decaying of America," *Newsweek*, August 2, 1982, p. 12.

[10]Associated General Contractors of America, p. 13.

[11]Ibid., p. 14.

[12]*Business Week*, "State and Local Government in Trouble," October 26, 1981, p. 135.

[13]Ibid., p. 137.

[14]Associated General Contractors of America, p. 15.

[15]Choate and Walter, *Ruins*, p. 3.

[16]Rochelle Stanfield, "The Users May Have to Foot the Bill to Patch Crumbling Public Facilities," *The National Journal*, November 27, 1982, p. 2016.

[17]Associated General Contractors of America, p. 10.

[18]Choate, "Wednesday," p. 1.

[19]*Business Week*, "State and Local Government in Trouble," Special Report, October 26, 1981, p. 63.

[20]Stanfield, p. 2021.

[21]David Lewis, et al., *Public Works Infrastructure: Policy Considerations for the 1980s*, (Washington, DC: Congressional Budget Office), 1983, p. 8.

[22]Ibid., p. 25.

[23]Pat Choate and Susan Walter, "Public Facilities: Key to Economic Revival," *The AFL-CIO American Federalist*, August 1981, p. 3 (hereafter cited as Choate and Walter, "Facilities").

[24]Robert W. Edgar, "Capital Budgeting: Taking Charge and Taking Control," Testimony before the Task Force on Budget Reform of the House Committee on Rules (Washington, DC: mimeo), 1982, p. 4.

[25]CONSAD Research Corporation, *A Study of Public Works Investment in the United States. Executive Summary*, (Washington, DC: U.S. Department of Commerce), 1980, p. 5.

[26]See Comptroller General of the U.S., *Effective Planning and Budgetary Practices Can Help Arrest the Nation's Deteriorating Public Infrastructure*, (Washington, DC: U.S. General Accounting Office), 1982.

[27]John E. Petersen and Wesley C. Hough, *Creative Capital Financing in the State and Local Sector: Causes, Characteristics, and Concerns,*" (Washington, DC: Government Finance Research Center), 1982, p. 1 (hereafter cited as Petersen and Hough "Creative").

[28]See Clinger.

[29]See Choate and Walter, "Facilities."

[30]See George E. Peterson et al., *America's Urban Capital Stock*, vols. 1–6 (Washington, DC: U.S. Department of Commerce), 1979–1981, p. 5, (hereafter cited as *Stock*); CONSAD; Comptroller General of the U.S.

[31]National League of Cities/U.S. Conference of Mayors, *Capital Budgeting and Infrastructure in American Cities: An Initial Assessment,* (Washington, DC: NLC/USCM), 1983, p. iv.

[32]John E. Petersen and Deborah Matz, *Trends in the Fiscal Condition of Cities: 1980–1982,* (Washington, DC: Joint Economic Committee, U.S. Congress), 1982, pp. 3–4.

[33]National Association of State Budget Officers and the National Governors' Association, *Fiscal Survey of the States: 1983,* (Washington, DC: National Governors' Association), 1983, p. 1.

[34]Associated General Contractors of America, p. 1.

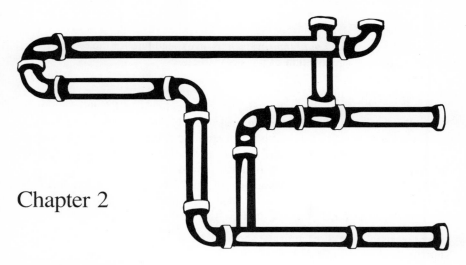

Chapter 2

THE BUDGET CONNECTION

The provision of public facilities and services for the benefit of all citizens traditionally has been considered a central function of state and local governments. Over the years these governments have developed a variety of approaches to allocate their resources and spend funds for capital purposes. The methods are as varied as the governments that use them.

This chapter will look at the processes used by state and local governments to identify, analyze, and select public capital projects. It describes three basic techniques commonly used by state and local governments to allocate capital—capital improvements programming (CIP), capital budgeting, and comprehensive/strategic planning. The CIP process is emphasized, because it has been the traditional vehicle for identifying capital projects, estimating costs, assigning priorities, and involving the public in project selection and financing. A summary of recent research on capital investment procedures by state and local governments, which concludes the chapter, emphasizes the concern about the general lack of attention paid to analyzing alternative methods of financing public facilities.

Capital Allocation Techniques

To facilitate a discussion of techniques employed in the capital allocation process, it is important to first define certain basic terms.[1]

Capital Outlay or *Capital Expenditure* refers to any spending made to purchase a physical asset that is expected to provide services over a period of time, usually at least more than one year.

Capital Project or *Capital Improvement* is an expenditure for the construction, purchase, or major renovation of physical structures.

Capital Improvements Programming is the selection and multi-year scheduling of public physical improvements.

Capital Budgeting is the annual process of deciding which public improvements listed in the CIP are to be funded and analyzing the various methods of financing such projects, along with their impact on the regular operating budget.

Comprehensive Planning is the process of developing a long-range plan for future land use. It is used chiefly by local governments.

Strategic Planning is the development of basic long-term strategies that seek to make the best use of existing and current resources, while limiting the impact of internal and external negative forces.

In a textbook world, each of the above elements would be an integral part of state or local government's capital allocation process. For example:

- The comprehensive plan, at the local level, spells out broad policies and objectives for community expansion and/or containment over a relatively long period of time.
- The capital improvement programming process, moving from general goals and guidelines, identifies in detail the type, location, and cost of the public improvements needed to serve the existing and future population and activity of the community.
- The capital budgeting process provides the funding for specific capital projects. It assesses the various methods of raising revenues and identifying the impacts of these costs on existing and future residents.
- Strategic planning (often at the state level) develops critical benchmarks of where the entity should be heading in broad areas such as economic development, job creation, environmental protection, transportation, etc., and—thereby—providing direction to the state legislature and state agencies in the preparation of the annual capital budget.

The environment for applying capital allocation techniques is fraught with political, bureaucratic, managerial, and social considerations in addition to the clearly fiscal and economic factors. In the real world, the development and implementation of public policy for allocating resources is not a tidy process, and the above scenarios describing state and local government capital planning rarely occur in such clear-cut or all-inclusive contexts.

The Capital Improvements Plan (CIP)

The capital improvement programming and budgeting process, as typically practiced by local governments, is summarized below.

Forms and instructions for preparing capital project proposals, developed by a central staff agency such as the planning department, finance department, or the office of the city manager/chief administrative officer, are issued to all operating departments. At the same time, a set of general budget guidelines depicting the locality's financial condition is prepared by the finance department and released by either the chief executive or the legislative body. These guidelines incorporate estimates and forecasts of expected own-source revenues such as property taxes, user charges and fees, and external funding sources such as federal and state aid.

Each operating department submits to a central review group its capital project requests and justification with cost estimates, information on projected effects on the operating budget, and proposed multi-year scheduling. A ranking or rating of projects usually is assigned by the submitting agency.

Project requests are compiled, and the central review group undertakes an assessment based on a set of evaluative criteria. These vary in accordance with the needs and policies of each jurisdiction.

The evaluative criteria are used to assess the various project requests and are applied in a priority-setting process. For evaluation purposes, some jurisdictions separate projects that are to be funded by "enterprise" or public utility revenues from those financed out of the general fund.

On the basis of this assessment, the review group submits to the chief executive or the legislative body its proposed capital improvement program. This document outlines the committee's recommended schedule of public improvements to be undertaken over a multi-year period—usually four to six years—with higher priority projects suggested for funding in the first few years of the CIP. Those projects recommended to be funded during the first year of the CIP comprise the proposed annual capital budget. The proposed CIP and capital budget, along with supporting documentation, are then reviewed by the chief executive and the governing body for modification and adoption. This entire process is generally institutionalized with a calendar, policies, instruction and guidances, and standard forms.

Benefits of a CIP

Developing a multi-year capital plan and budget can be a complex, time-consuming, and frustrating process, but local governments that make the effort have noted the following benefits.

1. A capital improvement program allows for the orderly repair and re-placement of capital facilities and equipment.
2. A CIP enables governments to collect useful information on the condition of their capital plant, to use these data to identify capital and maintenance needs, and maintain current inventories of capital assets.
3. Multi-year capital plans serve as the critical link between a government's goals, objectives, and outputs, and its anticipated revenues or resources.
4. A CIP assists government officials to work out priorities between current and future development, identify needs and wants, and decide whether to rebuild or replace existing capital infrastructure.

5. A CIP is a valuable financial planning tool. The process calls for a forecasting of own-source revenues, borrowing power, and intergovernmental assistance to estimate the level of capital spending that the government can safely afford over the next several years. The financial programming built into the CIP can help to:
   - smooth out the tax rate;
   - maintain a balance between debt service and current expenditures; and
   - determine debt capacity and debt service levels.
6. The process identifies capital projects several years ahead of actual need. This helps set aside adequate time for planning and design, and may enable governments to buy land, if necessary, on favorable terms.
 7. The process is a useful way to gain intergovernmental assistance to address identified capital projects.

Recent Research Findings

What has research revealed about the experiences of state and local governments in developing multi-year capital plans? Recent research efforts that provide insights into the application of capital allowance theories and methods by state and local governments are outlined in this section.

During 1977–1980, the American Society of Planning Officials and its successor, the American Planning Association (APA), in conjunction with the Municipal Finance Officers Association, looked at local government practices in the capital allocation process.[2] The study, *Local Capital Improvements and Development Management*, included an extensive literature search and six case studies of capital allocation practices in growing and declining communities.

APA's chief findings were that the capital allocation process as a tool to control the timing of growth was of limited effectiveness. Researchers found instances of communities faced with strong development pressures where developers were willing to move ahead and pay for the necessary facilities.

The study also demonstrated that the relationship between the comprehensive plan and the capital improvement plan varies widely—in some cases, the CIP explicitly describes the linkages between projects and plans, but in others it consists simply of a public "wish list." However, even the best thought out priority-setting procedures with high levels of staff and citizen participation were often governed by outside forces such as federal/state mandates and funding sources.

Finally, the APA research pointed to a major gap between the literature and practice concerning the analysis of alternative capital financing methods. The analysis was usually limited to such general terms as "pay-as-you-go" versus "pay-as-you-use" financing. Both the researchers and the case-study communities appeared to place a high degree of confidence on the viability of debt financing as a source of funds. The study was completed prior to the time when inflation, tight monetary policies, and federal tax changes sent the national municipal bond market into a period of record yields and volatile prices.

In the fall of 1982, the Urban Institute released the initial results of a research project that surveyed the capital investment priority-setting processes in 25 municipalities.[3] The Institute found that most (84 percent) of the cities have a five- or six-year capital improvement plan, and that in many cities, the first year of the plan is made the annual capital budget. However, some cities see the CIP as merely a public works "wish list" that has limited influence on the annual capital budget.

The Institute's report identifies specific aspects of the capital allocation process and establishes the frequency and nature of their uses by these city governments. The types of ranking or prioritizing are quantified in this research, as are the kinds of capital improvement review committees, the systematic use of evaluative criteria, and the forms of citizen participation in the process.

The Urban Institute's interim conclusions reiterate the APA study's finding that there are a wide variety of organizational arrangements in use with little evidence that any one arrangement is superior to any other. The study points to the need to utilize more specific information on proposed capital projects, including an assessment of infrastructure condition and alternative maintenance strategies. Also emphasized is the need for local governments to develop procedures to examine systematically alternative solutions to capital projects and to consider life cycle costs of various alternatives.

The U.S. General Accounting Office (GAO) report of November 1982, *Effective Planning and Budgeting Practices Can Help Arrest the Nation's Deteriorating Public Infrastructure*, is the most recent in a series of GAO studies of capital budgeting. It presents a broad analysis of the condition of America's capital plant, along with an assessment of how federal, legislative, and voter actions affect physical capital financing.

GAO surveyed four cities, five counties, four states, and one regional authority to review their strategies for managing capital assets. It concluded that four elements—assessing, planning, selecting, and controlling—are necessary in order for governments to successfully manage their capital assets and develop and maintain an infrastructure policy. The GAO found that some activities are common to governments with a successful capital allocation process:[4]

- collection of information on a periodical basis—concerning the condition of capital assets and the use of this information to identify maintenance needs and new capital items;
- development and application of guidelines or standards to assess the condition of the capital plant;
- preparation of multi-year capital plans covering at least five years;
- consideration of the long-term costs and benefits before making capital investment decisions;
- selection of projects based on need rather than availability of funds;
- establishment of priorities for long-range capital improvements during the planning and budgeting process; and

- review on a continuous basis of the status of ongoing capital projects to ensure that the previously established targets of time, money, scope are being met.

The Council of State Planning Agencies (CSPA) has published a series of reports in recent years on the subjects of state development policy and governance. Two of these focus on state capital budgeting and planning practices and their impacts on economic development—*The Capital Budget*, by Robert Devoy and Harold Wise, and *The Game Plan: Governance With Foresight*, by John B. Olsen and Douglas E. Eadie.

Devoy and Wise assert that investment in public facilities by state governments serves an increasingly pivotal role in fostering or maintaining economic development. Looking at capital budgeting practices in six states, the authors outline the major components of a state capital budget, the process of its development, and the economic consequences of state capital expenditures. They emphasize the assessment of the locational requirements and choices of business. Their list of suggested actions for bringing together the processes of state capital budgeting and economic development includes:

- upgrading the capital budget;
- expanding opportunities for various economic interests to influence capital budget decisions;
- reviewing the economic impact of state (and local) expenditures;
- spelling out the state and local facility and program requirement of each economic development policy; and
- assigning to one staff person the responsibility for the central preparation of the capital budget and economic development planning/research.[5]

The Game Plan, the first of a CSPA series on state governance, describes the application and benefits of strategic planning by state governments. Strategic planning and management, the authors say, are widely used by the private sector. They offer great potential for state governments both for an improvement in operations and an enhancement of the decision-making capabilities of governors, legislative bodies, and department managers. This CSPA analysis focuses on the adaptation of the largely private sector-oriented theory and practice of strategic planning to the unique needs and requirements of state governments. Moving from the theoretical to the practical, it presents detailed guidance on an incremental approach to the implementation of strategic planning by state governments.

Summary

This review of the processes that state and local governments use to identify, analyze, and select capital projects has described the basic procedural techniques that comprise the capital allocation process. By and large, the capital allocation process applied by states and by local governments uses similar techniques.

Undertaking such a process can provide governments with many benefits. Used properly, it can be a method for meeting replacement, repair, and new capital needs; a link between long-range plans and anticipated revenues, and a vehicle for garnering outside resources to meet capital needs.

Recent research on capital programming and budgeting efforts by the states and localities that was reviewed in this chapter suggests that a wide gap often exists between the theories that govern the capital allocation process and its implementation in the field. A number of factors, not the least among them the inherent political nature of the process, often force a compromise and a reassessment of how public funds for capital purposes should be spent. Only in a few cases do governments undertake a detailed assessment of proposed capital projects using a set of evaluation criteria to judge all proposed public improvements. Limited attention appears to be given to the analysis of alternatives to proposed capital projects.

Much attention has been focused on the assessment and selection of capital projects while much less effort has been applied to an analysis of how best to pay for them. As we review in the next chapter, the rapid rise in federal assistance in the decade of the 1970s skewed much of the capital planning and budgeting process toward those projects that would be recipients of "free" or "inexpensive" grant funds. Where projects needed to be financed in part out of state or local governments' own resources, the longevity of most capital projects has forced a strong bias toward debt financing as the "only" equitable alternative. The result is that few state and local governments undertake a sound analysis of different financing techniques. Such an analysis will need to be much more sophisticated than in years gone by because of the rapid changes occurring in the fiscal circumstances of governments at all levels and in the capital markets. The analysis of alternatives will typically begin with traditional debt financing alternatives. But, as we will document in the following chapters, the examination will consider that as a point of departure to a large number of alternatives the relative attractiveness of which will be conditional to the governments' economic and fiscal circumstances and prospects and the shifting needs and concerns of private investors.

Endnotes

[1] Adapted from A. John Vogt, *Capital Improvement Programming: A Handbook for Local Government Officials*, (Chapel Hill, NC: Institute of Government, University of North Carolina) 1977.

[2] See American Society of Planning Officials, *Local Capital Improvements and Development Management*, 4 vols., (Washington, DC: U.S. Department of Housing and Urban Development) 1980.

[3] See Harry P. Hatry, Annie P. Millar, and James Evans, *Capital Investment Priority Setting Process in Local Governments*, (Washington, DC: The Urban Institute) 1982.

[4] GAO defines a successful organization as one that is able to acquire or maintain capital stock, even under adverse conditions, without jeopardizing its mission or clientele.

[5] Robert DeVoy and Harold Wise, *The Capital Budget*, (Washington, DC: Council of State Planning Agencies) 1979, p. 26.

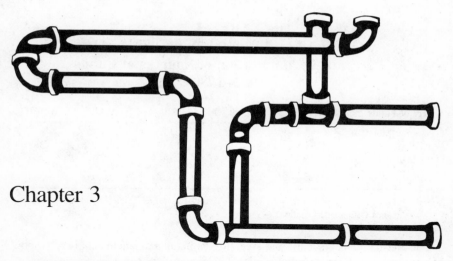

Chapter 3

THE FINANCE CONNECTION

The variety of alternatives available to finance public infrastructure improvements for economic development is rich in both traditional and creative financing techniques. The traditional wellspring of funds—the municipal bond market—is but one source among many. Under the right circumstances, creative methods of financing such as lease-financing techniques, tax increment financing, and pension fund investment financing can be tapped singly or in combination. Institutional arrangements such as special districts and public-private economic development ventures add another dimension to the growing list of possibilities.

A capsule description, in non-technical language, of the various financing approaches and arrangements cited above and a discussion of their major features, advantages, and limitations are offered in the following pages. Table 3 shows the increasing reliance of state and local governments in the mid- to late-1970s on federal grants to finance their capital spending. This reliance has created vulnerability.

Budgetary cutbacks at the federal level are withdrawing a major source of capital funds and as a result, state and local governments are forced to rely more heavily on current revenues or more debt financing. On the current revenues side of the equation, the prolonged fiscal pressures brought on by the wave of home-grown tax expenditure limitations (which has tainted and made difficult resource allocations to government) and several years of sluggish economic growth (which have depressed current revenues) have strictly limited that source of funds. In fact, demands on current budgets to keep operating with insufficient revenues have restricted capital spending even further. This has been done by reallocating funds to current revenues that otherwise would have been spent for capital purposes.[1]

TABLE 3
State and Local Capital Outlay Financing
Percentage Composition of Sources of Funds
1952-1980

Source of Funds	1952–57	1960	1970	1977	1980
Long-term Debt	56.0%	37.1%	51.0%	43.3%	37.0%
Federal Aid	8.5	20.0	22.0	32.1	36.0
Other Sources	35.5	42.9	27.0	24.6	27.0
TOTAL	100.0	100.0	100.0	100.0	100.0

Source: John E. Petersen and Wesley C. Hough, *Creative Capital Financing*, (Chicago: Municipal Finance Officers Association) 1983, p. 12.

The alternative is that state and local governments must increasingly rely upon borrowing to meet their capital needs. But, many of the same economic circumstances that led to the deterioration of support for capital spending from federal grants and current revenues have also created very unattractive credit market conditions. This makes borrowing a volatile and expensive means of raising funds for capital projects. It is the adverse conditions in the financial market— against the background of unmet capital needs, both public and private, and scarce resources on the current accounts—that form the basis for the surge of creative activity in the realm of state and local finance.

The next several sections discuss traditional as well as non-traditional debt market instruments. (See Table 2 for a summary of these instruments.)

Traditional Long-Term Techniques

The traditional method for a state or local government to obtain funds for capital investment has been to issue long-term bonds which mature 20 to 30 years from the date of issuance. In general, a bond issue's maturity should approximate the useful life of the asset being financed. Just as 20-year bonds should not be used to finance the purchase of police vehicles, short-term debt (with a maturity of one year or less) cannot be the final source of financing for wastewater treatment facilities. In other words, long-term needs should be financed, as much as possible, with long-term debt (bonds).

Bonds are generally classified as general obligation bonds (G.O.) and revenue bonds. The full faith and credit backing on a G.O. bond means that the property taxing power of the issuing government provides the credit support for the issue. In the event of default, investors have the ability to force the issuing authority to levy additional taxes to meet debt service payments. As a result, only those governments with taxing authority may issue G.O. bonds.

Revenue bonds are secured by the revenues of a particular enterprise, such as sewerage charges, highway or bridge tolls, or rental income from a building. An issuer pledges revenues from a project to support debt service and agrees to

TABLE 4
State/Local Capital Financing Techniques

	General Obligation Bonds	Revenue Bonds	Short Term Borrowing
Description	Traditional "plain vanilla" bonds backed by the full faith and credit of the issuing unit of government. The bonds are secured by an unconditional pledge of the issuing government to levy unlimited taxes to retire the bonds.	Principal and interest on the bonds are payable exclusively from the earnings of a public enterprise such as water or sewerage systems. No taxes are levied or pledged as a back-up.	Short-term borrowing instruments with maturities generally less than one year such as bond, tax, or revenue anticipation notes. Tax revenues or future bond proceeds pledged as security.
Purpose	Used by governments to finance capital projects which exhibit communitywide benefits that should be paid for by present and future residents.	To provide front-end financing for facilities that can pay for themselves over the investment's useful life from project revenues.	To take advantage of lower short-term interest rates at start of project. Also used to manage cash-flow requirements.
Market Acceptance	Traditional, well-known form of tax-exempt borrowing.	Highly dependent on service or project to be financed. Greater risk than for general obligation bonds.	Notes purchased by investors unwilling to commit long-term funds.
Advantages	• Due to strong security features, the interest rates of G.O. supported bonds are generally the lowest available. • More marketable debt due to higher security. • Opportunity to invest proceeds of bond issue.	• Credit analysis is straightforward. • Users pay for facility. • Default on issue does not burden local tax payers. • Usually no need for bond referendum. • Often not subject to debt ceiling. • Promotes sound financial management.	• Can be sign of astute financial management. • Ability to lower total project costs through lower interest costs. • Short-term borrowing generally does not require voters' approval though subsequent long-term bond sale may.
Disadvantages	• Credit analysis is complex. • May require voter approval. • May create need to raise taxes. • Time lags increase construction costs. • Subject to debt ceiling. • If paid by property taxes, cost of facilities may not be paid for by project beneficiaries.	• Generally higher interest costs. • Bonds usually contain restrictive covenants which may restrict operations. • Market for such debt is not as broad as for G.O. bonds.	• Threat of becoming overburdened with short-term debt. • Increases issuer's risk for the use of bond anticipation notes assumes that long-term rates will fall.

TABLE 4
State/Local Capital Financing Techniques (Continued)

	Compound Coupon Bonds	Zero Coupon Bonds	Variable Rate Bonds
Description	Long-term securities sold at par. Semi-annual interest accrues to investor at a compounded rate but is not paid until maturity.	Bonds that pay no interest prior to maturity. They are sold at a substantial discount from their face value, similar to a U.S. Government Series E savings bond.	Floating rate security wherein the interest rate is tied to one or more market interest rates, such as a percentage of the Prime Rate or U.S. Treasury Bill rate. The bonds or notes usually have a specified floor and ceiling on the rates. The cost of borrowing becomes variable rather than a fixed cost to the issuer.
Purpose	Similar to zero coupon bonds; allows issuer to defer interest payments until maturity. Lowers interest costs.	To lower interest costs to issuers and enable them to defer interest payments on the obligation until maturity.	To obtain lower interest rates by assuming a share of the investor's market risk.
Market Acceptance	Issuer assumes investor's reinvestment risk.	Investors value the ability to "lock in" a fixed rate of return as reinvestment risk is borne by issuer.	Popular with investors in a volatile market for the floating rate preserves the market value of the bond.
Advantages	• Lowers interest costs to issuer. • All debt service deferred until maturity. • Reduced administrative costs. • Investors guaranteed a fixed yield to maturity.	• Lowers interest costs to issuers. • Payment of interest is deferred. • Investors guaranteed a fixed yield to maturity. • Low initial investment popular with individual investors.	• Lowers interest costs to issuers. • Allows issuers to sell bonds to a broader market. • Investor's capital value of bonds is protected.
Disadvantages	• Balloon payment at end must be planned for by establishing a sinking fund. • High cost of calling in bonds for redemption prior to maturity.	• Some states may prohibit deep discounting of bonds. • Issuers receive much less cash up front. • May be difficult concept to sell to the public. • The balloon payment may increase credit risk. • Legal question of debt limit calculation may inhibit sale.	• Issuers face great uncertainty in debt service planning. • Requires greater expertise in administration.

TABLE 4
State/Local Capital Financing Techniques (Continued)

	Put Option Bonds	Bonds with Warrants
Description	A long-term bond which provides the investor the option of redeeming the issue well in advance of the stated maturity. The "put" creates a potentially shorter term obligation.	A warrant is a feature that provides the investor with an option to purchase additional bonds at a specified interest rate during a specific period.
Purpose	Lowers the cost of borrowing as long-term issue has characteristics of a short-term obligation.	To provide issuers with a method for lowering initial interest costs.
Market Acceptance	Investors value liquidity and protection from a major drop in market value.	Investors are willing to accept a lower rate of interest on the premise that interest rates will decline in the period for which the warrant is valid.
Advantages	• Lowers interest costs to issuers. • Allows issuers to sell bonds to a broader market.	• Lowers interest costs to issuers. • Warrants may be detached from bonds and sold separately, creating new market. • Broadens market for debt to include speculative purchasers.
Disadvantages	• May require back-up credit from a major financial institution. • Increases level of uncertainty in debt service planning. • Significnat risk exposure in having sufficient funds available to redeem debt if put is exercised.	• Issuer must be prepared to issue additional bonds. • If warrants are exercised, issuer must pay higher than prevailing interest rate.

TABLE 4
State/Local Capital Financing Techniques (Continued)

	Industrial Development Bonds	Tax-exempt Commercial Paper
Description	Bonds issued for private and quasi-public endeavors. They are secured by revenues of the bond-financed property.	Extremely short-term promissory notes with average maturity of 45 days. Notes are intended to be rolled over continuously for periods that may exceed one year.
Purpose	Used by governments to provide lower cost financing to promote industrial and commercial development.	Lowers borrowing costs to issuers with continuous need for short-term funds.
Market Acceptance	Very popular investments; high volume.	Preferred by investors concerned with rapid liquidity. Tax-exempt money market funds are large purchasers.
Advantages	• Provides low cost financing. • More marketable due to high yield offered investors. • May be useful to attract investment for economic development.	• Interest rates are lowest available. • Relatively easy to increase amounts outstanding. • Maturities may be tailored to specific needs of issuer or investor.
Disadvantages	• Public purpose of some IDB issuances causes questions. • IDBs may crowd out other demands on municipal market.	• High initial costs. • Requires daily staff commitment. • Letter or line of credit necessary. • Generally accepted $25 million minimum.

maintain rates and charges at a level adequate to cover future debt service. Since the source of funds to retire revenue bonds is generally considered riskier than property taxes, interest rates on revenue bonds are usually slightly higher than those of G.O. bonds issued by the same jurisdiction.

The volume of traditional tax-exempt bonds continues to increase although recent figures show a slight decline in long-term debt between 1980 and 1981 and an increase in short-term debt. However, 1982 posted record highs in both long- and short-term debt issuances and annualized data as of the second quarter 1983, show this trend is continuing. The following table provides comparative figures.[2]

	1980	1981	1982	1983p
	(dollars in billions)			
Long-term debt	47.1	46.1	77.2	102.4
Short-term debt	26.5	34.4	43.4	45.6
Total	73.6	80.5	120.6	148.0

p-preliminary date.
Sources: Government Finance Research Center, *Resources in Review*, Vol. 4 No. 6 and Vol. 5 No. 4.

Through the issuance of industrial development bonds (IDBs), governments sell tax-exempt revenue bonds and channel the funds from the sales into private and quasi-public endeavors. IDBs have become a large part of the tax-exempt bond market, although an accurate volume figure is not possible to develop, since most are placed privately. Estimates, however, range to a total of $8.4 billion in 1980 from approximately $24 million in 1969.[3] Because of the tax-exempt nature of the bonds, IDBs have financed businesses between 4 and 7 percentage points below the cost of conventional financing.[4]

Industrial development bonds have their share of critics who argue that they abuse the constitutional rights to tax exemption and that many of the facilities they finance (such as fast food restaurants and discount stores) serve little public purpose. As a result of these arguments, Congress, over the years, has imposed a variety of restrictions, including the creation of "exempt activities" and the "small issue exemption." The current small issue exemption allows the issuance of IDBs of $10 million or less; exempt facilities such as sewage treatment facilities, pollution control facilities, hospitals, airports, mass transit vehicles and housing (with qualifications), can be financed by issuances of more than $10 million. The most recent restrictions on IDBs were enacted by the 1982 Tax Equity and Fiscal Responsibility Act and include:

- the elimination of the tax-exempt status of small issue obligations issued after 1986;
- the elimination of the tax-exempt status of obligations issued after December 31, 1982, when more than 25 percent of the bond proceeds are

used for a facility primarily providing retail food and beverage services, automobiles sales or service, or the provision of recreation or entertainment; and

- the requirement that public approval be obtained for any IDB financing.

Despite the detractors, IDBs have many supporters among local officials who argue that IDBs attract new industry and that such incentives may be less costly than other types of development options. The new industry may also develop more jobs and increase the local tax base, supporters argue.

Another type of security that is often issued to finance major capital facilities such as wastewater treatment facilities is the special assessment bond. These bonds are similar to revenue bonds in that specific revenues are targeted to retire the debt. However, the bonds may carry the limited G.O. pledge of the issuer. Use of special assessment bonds often occurs when proposed facilities will benefit an easily distinguishable area or district. The bonds create a lien on only that property which benefits from the service.

Another financing instrument, called the "double barrelled" revenue bond, has two revenue sources pledged to its repayment. While the prime source of funds for repayment of these bonds is project revenues, the issuer also pledges its ability to levy taxes in the event that operating revenues are insufficient to meet debt service.

Creative Financing: What Is It?

In response to varying market demands and economic factors, issuers of municipal debt have become "creative." Just what this means in capital financing is highly judgmental. Most of the new techniques have been used in the taxable capital markets, but they usually have not been used to finance public capital expenditures. What is novel is the introduction of new loan instruments into the tax-exempt bond market or the creation of some new source of funds that had not previously existed and their consideration by state and local governments as alternatives in the raising of capital.

Creative financing is a "catch-all" term that implies a departure from standard practices: creative financing techniques are those that differ from the traditional means of raising capital through the sale of standard instruments in the tax-exempt securities market.

Creative financing techniques have dealt with the rearrangement of the borrowing transaction by shifting the risk of interest rate changes and, in some cases, of creditworthiness from the lender to the borrower. In addition, they have increased the types of returns available to the investor beyond the simple receipt of regular tax-exempt interest payments. An important aspect of the latter development has been the design of transactions in which governments are able to transfer certain tax benefits of ownership from themselves to taxpaying entities that can use them for tax-shelter purposes. Correspondingly, another related aspect of creative financing has been to devise ways by which governments themselves can take maximum advantage of financial investment opportunities through the temporary use of borrowed funds as a means of lowering costs. For both private investors and public borrowers, these aspects of creative financing are intimately connected to the peculiarities of the treatment of tax-exempt securities and depreciable assets in the federal tax code.

The following sections review several varieties of creative financing instruments.

Zero Coupon Bonds

Traditional bonds pay interest to the bondholder semiannually. The holder of a zero coupon bond, however, does not receive semiannual interest payments. Instead, the bonds are sold at a substantial discount from the par (face) value, similar to the U.S. Series E savings bonds. For example, a bond issued in 1982 which matures in 1994 with a par value of $5000 may be sold to investors at a price of $1250. At the issue's maturity in 1994, the government must pay the investor the bond's par value, $5000, at which time the imputed interest rate of 12.25 percent is realized. Due to the considerable value investors place on this type of issue, the interest rate is likely to be approximately 75 basis points (.75 percent) less than the issuer would have had to pay for a traditional bond with semiannual interest payments.

The appeal to issuers of zero coupon bonds is the lower interest cost. In addition, issuers can avoid some of the administrative costs that are associated with semiannual interest payments and, because the interest on the bonds is not paid until it is due in 10 to 25 years, the present value of the expense is much less than if the same dollar amount of interest had been paid throughout the bond's life. Investors like zero coupon bonds because they can "lock in" a fixed interest rate and also avoid some risk.

Among the disadvantages to the issuer of zero coupon bonds is that in order to realize, for example, $5 million in net proceeds, bonds with a total face value of $20 million or more may have to be issued. This discrepancy between par value and receipts may be difficult to explain to voters. The deferral of interest cost until the bonds' maturity can also create problems at the time of payment and should be planned for through the use of a sinking fund.

Because of these disadvantages, several variations on the theme of postponing interest until maturity have been developed. Among these are capital appreciation bonds, compound interest bonds, and municipal multiplier bonds. Like zero coupon bonds, all debt service payments on these bonds are deferred until maturity. However, the face, or par value of the bonds is their original purchase value, not their future value.

Put Option Bonds

One way that issuers can attract long-term investors while taking advantage of lower short-term interest rates, is to include a "put option" in the structure of the offering. A put option entitles the bond holder to return the bonds to the issuer at some future date prior to the bond's maturity. Two kinds of put structures have been used. Under the "window" put, the option can be exercised once during a certain period, e.g., on a specific day or month in the future. An "anniversary" put gives the investor the option to put the bond back to the issuer periodically, generally once every year.

Since investors view bonds with a put feature as a shorter term security than its intended maturity (considering the put option date as its real maturity), interest rates tend to be lower than on traditional long-term debt. In order to protect themselves and investors from the risk that a large number of put option bonds will be tendered at the same time, issuers generally must purchase "insurance" in the form of a bank letter of credit. This guarantees purchasers that there will be sufficient funds available to repay the bonds if the put feature is exercised.

The cost of the stand-by letter of credit and the risk that it may be called upon are the major disadvantages to the inclusion of a put feature. The advantage of put options is the lower interest cost. It is generally felt that the savings in interest cost (which has been estimated at 200 basis points)[5] offsets the expense of the letter of credit. A second advantage is that bonds redeemable at the option of the bondholder will be paid at par. When bonds are called in for redemption at the issuer's option, a premium of one percent to four percent generally must be paid.

Warrants

The term "warrant" in municipal finance has traditionally referred to a short-term security, often directly placed with a bank. The term has recently taken on a new identity analogous to its use in corporate financial markets, where warrant means an option to buy a stated number of shares of stock at a specified price. In the municipal market, warrants, which may be attached to bonds, permit the investor to purchase future bonds at the same price and coupon (interest) rate as the original issue. Including warrants in an issue should result in a lower interest rate because investor evaluation of the issue will include the value of the warrants in addition to the bonds' own value. By accepting a lower interest rate on bonds issued with warrants, the investor is betting on a decline in interest rates within the period for which the warrant is valid. If interest rates drop sharply enough to activate use of the warrants, the issuer must then sell bonds at a higher interest rate than is prevailing in the market. The decision to include warrants in an issue must be made in light of the expectation of future interest rate patterns. Issuers can limit their risk exposure by narrowing the period during which the warrants may be exercised.

Traditional Short-Term Borrowing Methods

Short-term borrowing is often used by financial managers as a daily, weekly, or monthly cash management tool. It enables municipalities to meet operating expenditures when revenue flows in only periodically as property or other tax revenues become due. Borrowing short-term through issuing notes or establishing a line of credit with a local bank can be a sign of astute management. Issuers of short-term debt must ensure, however, that what were intended to be only short-term obligations do not become long-term commitments through annual "rolling over" and eventual ballooning of short-term debt.

Another use of short-term borrowing has occurred in response to high tax-exempt interest rates for long-term obligations. In order to avoid making a long-term commitment at high rates of interest, municipalities have taken advantage of lower interest costs in the short-term market, with the intention of turning the short-term debt into a long-term obligation once market conditions improve. This use of short-term, interim financing permits project construction to begin on schedule even though long-term interest rates may be prohibitively high. This also can be a sign of prudent debt management as total interest costs for the project would be reduced. However, this use of short-term borrowing is generally considered to be less creditworthy than borrowing for temporary cash flow requirements since repayment is contingent upon the issuer's ability to gain access to the long-term market at a later date.

The most common traditional short-term instruments are Tax Anticipation Notes (TAN), Revenue Anticipation Notes (RAN) and Bond Anticipation Notes (BAN). Tax and revenue anticipation notes are refunded by tax or other revenues and are, therefore, primarily used for purposes of evening out cash flows, and not as interim project financing. Bond anticipation notes are securities traditionally issued as a bridge between the start of a project and eventual long-term financing. As short-term interest rates are generally lower than long-term rates, issuers may be able to lower total project costs through initial use of BANs, with eventual (in one to three years, depending on state laws and local charter) refunding by a bond sale, by which time it is hoped that long-term rates will have declined.

The major advantage of issuing BANs in lieu of long-term bonds is the lower interest rate. The issuer is making a gamble, however, that it will be able to gain access to the market at lower long-term rates when the notes mature. If rates do not decline appreciably, and if state laws or local charter do not prohibit it, the temptation to rollover the outstanding notes with another issue threatens to overburden the jurisdiction with short-term debt.

Creative Short-term Borrowing Methods

RANs, TANs, and BANs increasingly are being replaced by newer, less costly, and more flexible securities. One of the more visible new instruments, tax-exempt commercial paper, is specially tailored to cash flow purposes and is, therefore, usually issued in lieu of a TAN or a RAN. Up until quite recently, many bond counsels felt that Internal Revenue Service guidelines made the use of tax-exempt commercial paper for project financing very difficult. This view is changing, however, and potential issuers should discuss the matter with their bond counsel.

Tax-Exempt Commercial Paper

Tax-exempt commercial paper is similar to short-term debt that frequently is issued by corporations to finance their seasonal borrowing requirements. It differs from RANs, TANs and BANs in that the average maturity of the paper is between 30 and 45 days. The very short maturities make tax-exempt commercial paper a prime investment instrument for the tax-exempt money market funds. As there is very strong demand for such a liquid tax-exempt security, the interest rates on tax-exempt commercial paper are the lowest of all tax-exempt instruments. For example, rates quoted for top-quality, 30-day tax-exempt commercial paper in August 1982 reached a low of 4 percent when the rates on top-rated, one-year notes were approximately 7 percent.

The major disadvantage of tax-exempt commercial paper for municipalities is that in order to compensate for the high initial start-up costs of a tax-exempt commercial paper program, the minimum issue size should be about $25 million. Start-up costs include additional bond counsel fees, a bank letter of credit, and the fee charged by the investment firm which acts as dealer for the paper.

Variable or Flexible Rate Notes

Variable (also referred to as floating rate notes) and flexible rate notes are short-term obligations issued without a single, fixed interest rate. In the case of floating rate notes, the coupon rate is pegged to an index of one or more interest rates, e.g., the 3-month Treasury bill rate. The interest rate on flexible rate notes is not tied to another market rate, but is recalculated periodically by the issuer to reflect market rates. These instruments are similar, however, in that they both provide the issuer with a means of tapping the market at a lower cost than TANs, BANs or RANs. Investors are willing to accept a lower return from a flexible security that considerably reduces their market risk.

Variable and flexible rate notes generally have a "demand" feature included in the issue. This gives the investor the option to tender notes back to the issuer if the interest rate on the notes is unacceptable. Demand options are very similar to the put option discussed above in the long-term debt segment. The uncertainty that faces issuers is compensated for by lower interest costs than would be necessary with a fixed-term floating rate note.

The key to a successful floating rate issue is the index rate to which the note's interest is pegged. Careful selection of this rate is crucial, for it will determine the total issue interest costs. A variety of indexes can be used: a weekly or monthly average of the rates for other taxable or tax-exempt short-term notes, on similar average rates for taxable or tax-exempt bonds. In order to attract investors, the index must closely follow trends in other competing investments of similar risk and maturity. However, the more closely the index follows fluctuations in market rates, the more uncertain the total costs of the issue will be. While issuers may be tempted to minimize the variation, attempts to restrict the issue from market variation may result in the demand or put feature being exercised, thereby greatly increasing the issue's cost.

Issuers face a choice regarding the frequency with which the index is adjusted. Usually, either a weekly or monthly readjustment takes place unless a more stable market barometer, such as the prime rate, is chosen. Investors prefer the most frequent adjustment, which then makes the issuer more subject to swings in the market.

Nondebt Sources Of Capital

In recent years, increased attention has been paid to the use of nondebt methods for financing capital facilities. At present, a key alternative to bond financing that has gained widespread interest and use is leasing. Local governments lease finance capital purchases—such as firetrucks and computers—as well as office space and large communications systems. Recent changes in federal income tax laws have stimulated interest in leasing on the part of private investors and provide an opportunity for state and local governments to acquire the use of capital facilities at the least cost.

Leasing

Leasing is a way for municipalities to obtain capital facilities without issuing bonded debt. As lease obligations are not considered to be debt in most states, there is generally no requirement that voters approve the financing, nor is a community's debt limit a factor. There are several lease arrangements that municipalities can use to obtain all or part of necessary capital facilities.[6] The most familiar to local governments is the traditional operating lease. This arrangement is often used to acquire the use of office equipment and other moderately sized capital items without direct purchase. Other lease forms are tax-exempt financing leases, and sale-leasebacks. In all cases, a private investor, or group of investors that can use the benefits of either tax-exempt income or depreciation of the investment must be willing to enter into a contract with the municipality.

Two other lease arrangements which have been used successfully by municipalities are the tax-exempt lease purchase and the sale-leaseback. Each of these should be evaluated in light of both state and local restrictions on the sale and purchase of facilities and property as well as on the ability of the jurisdiction to incur financial obligations. In addition, the attractiveness of leasing to investors is primarily a function of the tax benefits they derive from the arrangement.

Tax-Exempt Lease Purchase

The tax-exempt municipal lease is a special form of a lease-purchase agreement wherein the interest component of the lease payments made by the municipality is considered by the lessor to be tax-exempt income. Any item of property or equipment which the supplier is willing to sell on an installment basis can be acquired in this manner. While lease-purchase arrangements often directly involve the actual manufacturer or distributor of an item, a third party, in the form of a commercial bank or a specialty lease-financing company, may enter into unusually large deals. In the latter case, the third party purchases the structure or equipment on the municipality's behalf, and then enters into a tax-exempt lease with the government. The third party may sell certificates of participation to interested investors who would share in the tax-exempt interest income.

If properly structured, the actual lease should not obligate the municipality to continue the lease beyond its current fiscal year. This is achieved by making the lease obligation contingent on annual appropriations by the governing body. The investors in the lease must, therefore, be convinced that the item is of necessity to the local government so that they will not back out before the leased item has been fully acquired. Because of this structuring of the lease, it is not considered to be debt, and, therefore, not subject to a community's debt limit or to voter approval. It is, however, important that the community recognize the lease obligation as a long-term commitment and, for planning purposes, treat it in the same way as long-term debt.

The greatest advantage of municipal lease purchasing is that it allows the locality to acquire an asset using long-term financing without technically incurring debt. In addition, the costs of entering into the lease agreement may be less than would be incurred if a bond referendum and subsequent bond issue were used. One major disadvantage to lease financing is that "debt service" (the annual or semi-annual lease payments) must be budgeted from current revenues. Bond referenda to approve G.O. debt often include a provision for an additional tax levy to cover necessary debt service.

Sale and Leaseback of Public Property

In a sale-leaseback arrangement, public property (generally a capital facility) is sold to private investors and some or all of it is then leased back for use by the local government. The lease must be structured as an operating lease, not a lease-purchase. The private owners are able to take advantage of federal tax incentives for investment, particularly depreciation of the property and, possibly, investment tax credits, if the arrangement involves renovation of the facility. The cost of the lease to the local government will reflect the private tax benefits and may, therefore, be less than the debt service expense if bonds were issued to renovate the facility.

The advantages of a sale-leaseback include the lower cost of renovating or converting a public building and the initial infusion of cash from the sale of property. Local governments typically invest the sale proceeds and use the interest income to subsidize the lease payments. One major obstacle to sale-leaseback may be citizen or political reluctance to allow the municipality to sell public property. While the local government may have first option to buy the property, it must be at a fair market value to be determined at the time of resale.

Other Financing Arrangements

Pension Fund Financing

Since public and private pension funds are the largest single source of capital in the United States today, representing 16.6 percent of all capital market investments, they are potentially a major source for infrastructure financing. There are an estimated 500,000 private pension plans, 6,600 state and local government pension plans, and 38 special federal worker retirement plans. Currently, private pension funds total $750 billion, while public pensions are valued at about $250 billion. Total assets of the top 100 plans are greater than the combined assets of the first 11 firms in the Fortune 500. Both types of funds are expected to grow significantly in the coming years. The Department of Labor estimates that pension funds in the private sector will be worth some $3 trillion by 1995.[7] The AFL-CIO estimates that state and local pension funds should grow to well in excess of $1 trillion during the same period.[8]

Due to their tremendous size, pension funds exert a major influence on the flow of investment capital. Historically, the portfolios of most pension funds have invested heavily in the stocks and bonds of major corporations, with over 90 percent of the common stocks they hold listed on the New York Stock Exchange, which lists the common stock of only 1,557 companies.[9] A number of factors have contributed to this conservative investment decisionmaking. Because larger firms are easier and more economical to research for investment information, and because many of the disclosure and reporting requirements imposed by the Securities and Exchange Commission often discriminate against smaller firms, it is frequently simpler for the funds to invest conservatively. However, the pivotal factor is the "prudent man" rule that specifies that fund managers must make investment decisions acting as a prudent man—using prevailing wisdom and market conditions—would in the investment of his own funds.

Managers must also act in the exclusive interest of plan beneficiaries, which generally is interpreted to mean investing in only the most liquid, readily recognizable, and "sound" investments—"blue chip" stocks and bonds and guaranteed, fixed-income government securities.[10] Since pension fund managers can, in certain circumstances, be held personally liable, their investment policies often explicitly restrict investments to "low risk" firms that have at least $50 million in assets and a strong history of annual dividends. As a result of such practices, pension funds now own one-fourth of all corporate stock outstanding in the country. According to a study by Peter F. Drucker, pension funds now own enough common stock to effectively control the 1,000 largest industrial firms in America and the 50 largest nonindustrial firms in the banking, insurance, retail, communication, and transportation sectors.[11]

Pension funds are now involved in a period of major transition and change. In recent years, the above practices have been increasingly questioned by a number of groups, including Congress, researchers, public interest groups, and plan beneficiaries. Pension fund managers have been criticized for the poor performance of most portfolios because the rate of return of most of their stock investments has consistently lagged behind returns enjoyed by the stock market as a whole. Returns on investment must be greater in order to limit the size of increases in contributions from employers and employees to meet future benefit outlays. This is becoming a critical issue for many seriously underfunded public pension systems whose governments are facing severe revenue shortfalls and high competition among existing expenditures.

Many recent research studies have argued that there are many opportunities for capital investments in small businesses, the housing market, and other sectors that would give both high investment yields and ensure the unimpeded provision of retirement benefits. Because of the long-term liquidity needs of pension systems, they can be a unique source of long-term capital for business and housing ventures and other development investments.[12]

"Socially beneficial" instruments by pension funds have become popular for several reasons including:

- the concerns of labor unions over pension fund investments in corporations investing overseas or in non-union enterprises; and
- the concerns of representatives from the Northeast and Midwest that their funds are being imported to other regions.[13]

A great deal of discussion and debate has occurred over what constitutes socially useful or development investments. In some cases, it means geographically targeting pension fund investments and it may involve setting aside a portion of pension funds for community-oriented projects such as neighborhood health clinics, day care centers, and low- to moderate-income housing. For others, social investing means making available funds that governments can use to construct public improvements to stimulate economic activity. For still others, it entails filling the "capital gap" by providing venture capital for small, young firms, which have great potential for creating many jobs, but are currently denied access to capital due to inefficiencies in the financial markets. Finally, the concept of social investing can mean the divesting of pension fund money from firms that have major investments in South Africa, or are anti-union.

While the debate over social investments in pension funds is still young, attempts have recently been made to address the issue. These include:

- In 1980, the Executive Council of the AFL-CIO adopted a broad set of policy recommendations for the investment objectives of union-negotiated pension funds. The recommendations call for union members to encourage the use of pension funds to: increase employment through reindustrialization, and advance social purposes such as worker housing and health centers.[14]

- A survey of public retirement pension systems conducted by the Government Finance Research Center early in 1983 found that 19 of the 130 systems surveyed (15 percent) targeted a total of $3.5 billion for investment thought to benefit a jurisdiction's economy. Included were investments designed to increase employment, finance local governments, and provide capital for small businesses. Most such investments were made by state and local systems with more than one million dollars in assets. Over half of the investments were made by systems located in the Northeast.

  The largest single targeted investment, $1.2 billion, was made by a large city retirement system in order to provide financing for its local government. Other targeted investments include $475 million to meet the housing needs of low- and moderate-income residents, $95 million to provide capital for small businesses, $73 million to revitalize urban areas, and $60 million to increase employment in declining regions.

  A large portion ($1.2 billion) of these investments was made through government securities offered by the Government National Mortgage Association, the Federal National Mortgage Association, and the Federal Home Loan Mortgage Corporation. Other investment vehicles included conventional mortgage backed securities ($244 million), Federal Housing Administration insured residential mortgages ($220 million), and Small Business Administration guaranteed loans ($5 million).[15]

- The Dreyfus Third Century Fund, a major institutional fund specializing in social investments, has consistently outperformed the stock market over the last five years. The fund recorded an increase of 180 percent over the five-year period ending March, 1980, compared to a gain of 33 percent in the Dow Jones Industrial Average.[16]

In seeking to attract pension funds to meet social needs and revitalize state and local economies, a number of different techniques have been utilized. These new portfolio investment strategies can be classified into two basic types: 1) direct private investment/lending and 2) federal and state developed instruments and incentives.

The first type involves the direct investment or lending of money to either communities or firms. Examples include investments in venture capital firms, and small business investment companies (SBICs), direct placement of corporate and private debt, purchases of over-the-counter stock, and the creation of pension fund investment pools.[17]

In most cases, pension funds have been attracted to these financing instruments due to their ability to provide a higher rate of return than lower risk investments such as publicly traded corporate stocks and bonds. Small business investment companies are increasingly attractive for pension fund investment due to their ability to leverage guaranteed low interest loans from the federal government. Direct placement of debt or equity enables pension funds to invest in the issues of smaller firms and to reduce the costs of underwriting. Pension funds generally insulate themselves from the higher risks associated with the above investments by counterbalancing them with more conservative, highly liquid investments such as U.S. Treasury bills and notes.

A major consequence of entering into these kinds of financing arrangements is that a much more sophisticated level of financial analysis is required. Venture capital, limited partnerships, and SBICs must be evaluated and selected from among numerous potential ventures. The structuring of deals requires expertise in a variety of financing arrangements such as common stock, preferred stock, convertible debt, and subordinated debt. Additional expertise is required to properly monitor investee performance and provide technical assistance when needed. A high level of skills and experience are also a necessary prerequisite to undertaking private placements or the purchasing of small company public equity issues through the over-the-counter stock market. While some pension funds are large enough to warrant an in-house capacity to purchase and manage such investments, many pension funds channel their investments through an insurance company or contract for such services with an investment banker or financial advisor.

New investment strategy also involves the use of public financial instruments and investments created and managed by the federal or state governments. Most states are involved in business development financing through a host of public loan and guarantee programs. Some of these are industrial revenue bonds, direct loan programs, state venture investment funds, and business loan guarantee/insurance programs. The federal government operates a loan guarantee program through the Small Business Administration. A similar set of investments has been developed to facilitate investment in housing finance, such as the creation of mortgage-backed pass-through securities. In some cases, the state or federal government is providing the institutional capacity to promote investments in economic development or housing. While pension funds are generally not investors in IDBs because of lower returns caused by their tax-exemption, they are increasingly attracted to investments in mortgage backed securities. Insurance or guarantee programs may provide the incentive for pension funds and other risk-averse investors to participate in financing riskier projects if a third party assumes at least part of the risk. Investment insurance can also reduce the management costs to pension funds and other investors by reducing the costs associated with monitoring the performance of a pool of housing or business loans.

As noted above, a variety of approaches has been applied to encourage alternative investments by pension funds. Some have been criticized for either displacing other sources of capital, or offering financial concessions that force the funds to accept below market returns. According to Lawrence Litvak, author of *Pension Funds and Economic Renewal*, displacement investment occurs when a pension fund invests in projects for which investors already exist.[18] A classic example of displacement, according to Litvak, is the investment by pension funds in government-guaranteed mortgages to stimulate housing finance.[19]

The pension field is an evolving one. Most of the new investment strategies tend to focus on directly stimulating economic development or meeting identified social needs. Generally, only a few examples exist whereby pension funds have been used by governments as a financing source for infrastructure projects. The most notable example is in New York City, where in 1975, the city's pension funds played an instrumental role in helping the city to ward off financial collapse by purchasing its securities. In that case, the City's tapping of pension funds was heavily contingent upon a number of financial guarantees as well as state and federal oversight. However, recent innovations hold the promise that financing arrangements can be structured with adequate safeguards that will involve pension funds in financing public improvements.

Public Enterprise

Self-supporting utilities and off-budget enterprises—increasingly popular arrangements for delivering public services—are public corporations created and owned by one or more political jurisdictions. They are usually referred to as authorities, districts, commissions, agencies, or boards. Commonly formed by a public statute that outlines their authority and powers, they operate separately from general purpose governments. In most states, establishment of a public enterprise is generally a routine procedure that requires the passage of a local ordinance and/or the filing of a corporate charter. Only in a few states, such as New York, is the chartering of certain public enterprises contingent upon special acts by the state legislature.[20]

Public enterprises generally finance the construction of capital projects with revenue bonds which are paid back through user charges and fees. The bonds usually contain restrictive covenants that not only require a minimum coverage ratio to meet debt service costs, but also mandate that the schedule of fees and/or charges accommodates a minimum level of maintenance and repair.

User charge or fee systems tend to vary with the type of services provided by the public enterprise. Revenue-raising methods include permits, licenses, and fines, connection and "tap-in" fees, benefit district assessments, systems development charges, front footage fees, and periodic (usually monthly) user charges.[21] In addition, in rapidly growing areas developers are often assessed added fees for the privilege of future tie-in of their properties into facilities operated by government corporations. Public enterprises, such as sewer facilities, may develop a schedule of charges and fees based on the quantity and quality of the wastewater, with surcharges assessed on strong industrial wastes. Public water systems may incorporate a rate schedule that either gives quantity discounts or levies higher charges to heavy users, depending upon whether water conservation or marginal cost pricing is to be encouraged. The underlying intent of most charge or fee systems is to fairly assign the cost of the service to the user. This "ability to pay" concept may cause differential service pricing between user classes, with industrial users often being levied higher charges than residential customers.

In recent years, both the number and type of public enterprises have proliferated. Traditionally, government enterprises were limited to public monopolies such as electric and gas utilities, or to single purpose districts which provided basic public services in unincorporated areas adjacent to cities. Today, government corporations operate a wide spectrum of facilities and services—from airports and university dormitories to parks and zoos. Functional categories include basic communities services, recreation and civic activities, transportation, drainage and resource conservation and several others. Their organizational structures range from small independent local authorities to statewide agencies. They usually enjoy powers of eminent domain that can extend beyond the political boundaries of the political entities that created them. Also, they are often exempt from federal and state regulations, as well as from antitrust laws regarding price fixing.[22]

A number of explanations have been given for the rapid growth and favorable acceptance of public enterprises. In some cases, general purpose governments have not been able to respond adequately toward new or expanded services requested by residents, and as a result, citizens often find it easier to establish a new district rather than have the service incorporated into the general budget. Special districts, especially in rural areas, are seen by many as being the most effective way to both deliver services and capture costs for the same. The growing interest in operating government as a business has also helped to spur the creation of public enterprises. Their acceptability is shown by a 1981 survey by the Advisory Commission on Intergovernmental Relations, that finds that there exist fairly strong positive public attitudes towards charging the user of government services rather than raising taxes for all citizens.[23]

While the above discussion explains some of the expanded uses of government corporations, critics say that state and local governments rely on public enterprises to bypass state-imposed restrictions on taxing, spending, and borrowing. They argue that these entities have been established to enable the issuance of bonds without voter approval, and to allow jurisdictions to raise revenues in light of voter imposed constraints on increases in property taxes and other taxes. Their growth has paralleled the taxpayers' revolt which occurred in many states during the 1970s.

The most significant impact of this growth in enterprises has taken place in the municipal bond market. Borrowing by special districts and public authorities during the 1970s has radically changed the structure of the tax-exempt securities market. In 1980, $34.4 billion, or 71 percent of long-term municipal securities sold were revenue bonds. This figure compares with 48 percent of all issues sold in 1975 and 34 percent in 1970.[24] As of 1975, revenue bonds issued by public authorities and special districts represented the largest single source of new state and local government security sales. Government corporations were responsible for 54 percent of all tax-exempt security sales in 1979, compared to just 31 percent in 1970. Data compiled by the U.S. Census Bureau show a significant increase in debt issued by "Special District/Statutory Authority" since 1975. While the voter-approved debt issued by cities, counties, and townships grew by 44 percent between 1974 and 1980, public enterprise debt increased by 172 percent. Meanwhile, the guaranteed debt issued by state governments actually declined by 9 percent for the same time period.[25]

Public enterprises have alternately been praised and criticized, with both sides pointing to the same features to support their respective arguments. Supporters cite the flexibility that government corporations have in raising revenues and financing capital needs. Public enterprises are not bound by local tax or spending limitations and they do not have to compete with other items in the annual budgets of general purpose governments. Since they are isolated from the political process, and have reliable sources of funding, public enterprises can focus on the provision of the types of services that are demanded by their customers. This observation indicates that public facilities operated by independent authorities are generally in better condition than those managed directly by local governments.

Critics argue that additional layers of government complicate the delivery of services, fragment the decision-making process, and lead to greater inefficiencies. The apolitical nature of government corporations and their tendency to be off-budget are seen as ways to circumvent the desire of taxpayers for a fiscally balanced public sector.

In light of the poor fiscal outlook of most state and local governments, public enterprises will probably continue to be relied upon as vehicles to provide essential services and for the construction of public facilities. As long as the public's perceptions of government corporations remain positive, greater application of these entities can be expected.

Tax Increment Financing

Local governments use tax increment financing (TIF), also known as tax allocation financing, as a mechanism for underwriting the public costs of improvements in the redevelopment of commercial and industrial areas by earmarking specific future tax revenues. Introduced by the State of California in 1951, tax increment financing was slow to spread to other states until the mid-1970s, when the end of federal grants for urban renewal forced local governments to seek other sources of financing for urban redevelopment. TIF is now used in approximately 20 states, and for a number of cities it has become a key method of financing new growth and increased private sector investment in blighted or declining areas.

Tax increment financing itself is not a tax, but is analogous to special benefit taxation. TIF captures the increases in assessed valuation of land and improvements that result from redevelopment and new construction in a specially created development district and reserves the ensuing increased property tax revenues (the tax increment) to meet the public costs associated with the development. In some cases, the tax increment revenues are pledged to repay debt issued to finance the development while in others, it is reserved for annual expenditure targeted to the project. The property tax base is "frozen" while the tax increment agreement is in effect, and during that time other entities with taxing authority in the district are precluded from sharing in the revenues that result from the increased value of the property. They do, however, continue to receive tax revenues from the district up to the frozen base level.

Sizeable investments are required in order to create a project which will generate sufficient revenues to make TIF work; therefore, TIF is often used as the framework for one or more financing instruments such as industrial development bonds, lease revenue bonds, community development block grants (CDBG), urban development action grants (UDAG), and private sector financing. Key elements in the success of a tax increment financing system are a thorough feasibility analysis that demonstrates that the benefits will exceed the costs, and the "up-front" commitment of a viable development company. A schematic representation of the tax increment flow expected to be generated by a development project is illustrated below.

While tax increments can be applied to redevelopment costs on an annual, pay-as-you-go basis, the more effective uses of TIF involve the pledging of tax increments as security for bonds or notes issued in connection with a project.[26] This is typically done through the sale of "tax allocation bonds" that are secured by the projected increases in property tax revenues. The marketability of this type of bond is highly dependent on the likelihood that a substantial increase in property values will result from the public improvements being financed by the bond proceeds. Interest on tax allocation bonds is higher than that on general obligation bonds due to the inherent risk and the fact that they are guaranteed only by the municipality's "moral obligation" rather than the full faith and credit that backs general obligation bonds.

FIGURE 1
Graphic Illustration of a TIF Redevelopment Project

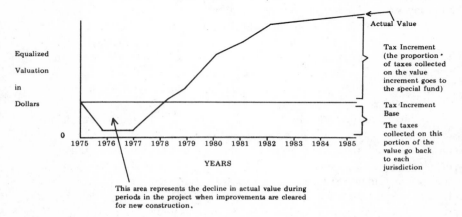

Source: Department of Local Affairs & Development, State of Wsiconsin.

Redevelopment of blighted areas—urban renewal—has been the most frequent objective of tax increment financing programs, and many states limit the availability of TIF to well-defined blighted areas. Extending the uses of TIF to encompass development as well as redevelopment is an issue under discussion in some states. It is seen as a method that would allow the local government to pay the public costs of development and complement state tax relief programs by offering an economic incentive to private investment.[27] The experience of Minnesota, which allows the use of tax increment financing not only for housing redevelopment but for rural and urban industrial and general economic development purposes as well, has been called a successful experiment by the National Council for Urban Economic Development.[28] The track record of TIF in that state may prove instructive as a case study.

In the wake of Proposition 13's limitations on local governments' taxing powers, which brought about severe constraints on local governments' borrowing abilities, California has devised a wide range of special assessment/special tax mechanisms for financing public infrastructure along with new development. The combination of traditional redevelopment tax increment financing with special limited tax obligation bonds, made possible under California's 1982 Mello-Roos legislation, offers a potential for funding the acquisition or leasing of capital improvements for cities, counties, school districts, and special police, fire, park, or recreation districts.[29]

Improvement Districts

Improvement districts, also known as special districts, have long been a traditional source of financing for public facilities. Since the turn of the century, special taxing districts have been established in both urban and rural areas to provide specific types of public imrpovement or service which is deemed to benefit a particular group of property owners. Early applications of improvement-district financing focused on street-oriented improvements such as street paving, street lighting, and sidewalks. Over time, the use of the device was expanded to include such services as flood control and drainage, ambulance service, insect and pest control, and transportation services for the elderly. However, in recent years, local officials have come to consider the use of improvement districts as an economic development financing tool and have used them to stimulate the revitalization of central business districts, commercial strips, neighborhoods, and historic preservation districts. The proceeds from these special assessments have been used to undertake a variety of projects such as free parking, street furniture, decorative lighting, plazas, outdoor malls, cultural centers, extra security, and commercial attraction or promotion activities.

An improvement district is a legal device for assigning the costs of public improvements to benefitted properties through the levying of special tax assessments. Districts are commonly established in two ways—either a city council or appropriate legislative body can pass an ordinance or resolution; or, property owners can have a particular area designated through an initiative petition.

Construction and financing of public improvements over a short period of time can be provided through improvement districts. Special assessment bonds can be sold to provide up-front financing of the costs of construction and maintenance. In addition, the device also enables property owners in the district to pay off the costs of improvements over a long period of time, usually 10 years. This is far more affordable than paying for total costs of public improvements on a one-time basis. Because the special assessment bonds are tax-exempt, the costs to individual property owners are generally less than private financing.

A key feature of an improvement district is its method of assessment. One commonly used method is to allocate the cost of district improvements according to a ''basis of assessment.'' This is a predetermined formula created from such predictable measures as linear front footage of the benefitted property, square footage of the property, or the average assessed valuation of land.[30] Additional criteria may be included such as the distance from the improvements, or the frequency of use.

Improvement districts have been popular financing vehicles because the property owners who pay for the improvements constructed in the district directly benefit from their contribution. The revenues generated from the assessments are exclusively used to retire the improvement bond(s) and meet the costs of providing the service. Taxpayers have been increasingly attracted to taxing methods that identify the type and amount of service or public improvement and that assign a dollar value to it.

Improvement districts are also an effective method of raising money to finance public improvements without tapping into general fund revenues. Finally, the long-term payback feature of special assessments minimizes the financial impact on individual property owners.

Improvement districts have been criticized for creating additional layers of government which may reduce the efficiency of delivering services. When an improvement district is formed adjacent to the political boundaries of a city, it may be difficult for the municipality to annex the district if it is already provided with such basic services as sewer and street maintenance. Meanwhile, because of the district's proximity to the city, its residents enjoy the many other services of the city without paying for them.

The manner in which assessments are levied can also create inequities. Assessments based on front footage tend to favor large, multistory buildings. Square footage formulas benefit smaller properties. Developing a formula that encourages economic development may impose an unfair burden on other property owners.

Public-Private Partnerships

A public-private partnership can be defined as ''any mutually beneficial activity undertaken by government and business to solve community problems that yields benefits to both the private interest and the community at large."[31] The widest applications and most visible successes of public-private ventures have been in the field of economic development. Decreasing federal assistance and increasing development costs have made it necessary for public-private sector sharing of the planning, financing, construction, and marketing risks associated with many economic development projects. By combining the best attributes of government and business, a number of highly acclaimed economic development projects have been assembled. Contributions by the local governments in these joint ventures have included the following:

- leveraging of state and federal grants such as urban development action grants (UDAGs);
- providing public improvements and support facilities;
- using financing arrangements and incentives such as industrial development bonds, tax increment financing, and tax abatements;
- using eminent domain to assemble large tracts of land for later sale to developers;
- underwriting the costs of relocation;
- approving zoning changes;
- accelerating the permit processes;
- preparing design and development plans; and
- selling air rights over and under public land.

The private sector has participated in these partnerships by:

- forming special business partnerships and advisory committees;
- undertaking detailed plans and feasibility studies;
- lending business executives to assist in financing and marketing;
- entering into special assessment arrangements; and
- assembling private sector financing.

In recent years, public-private partnerships have become an important source of innovative approaches to financing infrastructure improvements. The availability and adequacy of public facilities and services are an essential elements to the proper functioning of business organizations, because they directly affect the costs of doing business. The absence of a good public infrastructure can create an unbreakable barrier to plant expansion or relocation. Severe budgetary constraints have forced local governments to seek alternatives to the traditional role of providing public facilities and services in return for taxes and fees. In response to these concerns, many communities have entered into joint ventures with the private sector to facilitate the provision of public facilities and services. The three basic types of partnerships which have been developed are operating services, management assistance, and private construction or purchase of capital improvements.

The most common practice has been the "privatization" or contracting out of public services. Private delivery of services has proved cost effective in certain cases and many private firms have provided particular expertise in certain functional areas. In some situations, the public service and/or facility may become the total responsibility of private companies, such as the contracting out of rubbish collection services to private disposal firms. In other cases, private firms have been hired to supervise the operations of a public facility; for example, a private management team might run a wastewater treatment facility. The pros and cons of the private delivery of services need to be considered in each situation. Such factors as the cost and quality of the service, contractor performance, labor/management relations, legal restrictions, and the applicability of the service to private operations must all be taken into account.

Local governments have also tapped the personnel and support resources of private companies to supplement local government management of public facilities and services. The chief sources of private sector expertise have been major corporations and financial institutions. In some cases, staff from these firms have been "detailed" to work directly with government personnel to improve both the financial management and the operation of public facilities. This approach may include the use of company equipment such as computers, or the implementation of administrative procedures developed in the private sector. Another form of management assistance involves the formation of advisory committees and task forces composed of executives and experts from the business community. The assistance that these groups provide may vary but can include help to a government to identify and resolve fiscal problems in order to deliver an adequate level of public facilities and services, or the conduct of a study to identify infrastructure deficiencies that deter economic growth with suggestions for improvement.

Public-private partnerships have also been used to supplement public resources to provide capital facilities and improvements. In some cities, downtown businesses have agreed to assess themselves a fee to provide revenues to pay for landscaping, street furniture, decorative lighting, and other public improvements, along with all public operating and maintenance expenses. With the passage of the Economic Recovery Tax Act of 1981, many cities have entered into leasing arrangements with private investors. As previously mentioned, these joint ventures include the leasing of both transit vehicles and public buildings.

Public-private partnership is the new phrase being circulated as the solution to many community problems, including the deterioration of public works due to insufficient financing. The growing list of successful joint ventures lends credence to this positive outlook. The role of government as risk-taker and entrepreneur is an evolving one. The role of private business, especially large corporations, is becoming increasingly public in nature. However, while many partnerships have been highly successful, others have experienced problems with mismatched perceptions of timing and goals between public and private entrepreneurs. The key ingredients of partnerships that work are 1) recognition of mutual interests; 2) clear definition of roles and responsibilities; 3) development of feasible objectives; and 4) strong local leadership either from the private or public sector.

Additional Revenue-Raising Techniques

State and local governments have developed and applied a number of additional financing arrangements to meet public infrastructure needs. In these, government is still the traditional provider of public improvements, despite many of the public-private arrangements discussed earlier, but an innovative payment arrangement is utilized. Methods in this category include real estate transfer taxes, construction taxes, and systems development charges.

A real estate transfer tax, as the name implies, is a tax that is levied at the time real property is sold. It is usually calculated as a percentage of the sale price. If the tax is imposed each time there is a change in ownership, there are four points of application: 1) sale of vacant land, 2) sale of improved lot, 3) sale of land and buildings, and 4) resale of property.

A construction tax is a tax on building improvements collected at or near the time of occupancy. The tax is usually structured as a percentage of the value of the building permit. The tax collects revenues on multi-family, commercial, and industrial construction. Such structures are traditionally retained by the owners. Thus, the tax captures revenues not available through a real estate transfer tax.

A systems development charge is a program of levying charges and fees to allow new development to "buy into" the existing infrastructure and to help defer the costs of future public facilities. The fees can range from a few hundred to several thousand dollars and are usually levied at the time a building permit is obtained. Some communities impose one flat fee for all facilities, while others levy a series of charges for the park, street, water, sewer, and other utility systems. The charges are assessed in terms of a standard or a combination of standards such as building floor area, number of dwelling units, number of parking spaces or other such measures. Once a schedule of fees is established, the fees may remain at a fixed level or be triggered to increase with a measure such as the consumer price index.

All of these methods generally have been applied in areas experiencing rapid growth and strong public attitudes towards having the developers "pay their own way." Many public officials see the devices as a ready source of revenues, which are easy to administer, and usually do not require a vote of the electorate. Systems development charges have been criticized as an inequitable way of raising revenue for public improvements. The systems charge adds to the front-end cost of housing, thus making new housing less affordable to low- and middle income families.

Typically, the buyers of new housing have been long-time residents of the community, who have been "paying into" the capital plant for several years. Finally, the charges may be forcing purchasers of new housing to subsidize general systems improvements which benefit the community as a whole. A real estate transfer tax helps to alleviate the problem by having all properties share in the costs of public improvements, which includes new facilities and the repair and replacement of the existing capital plant.

Summary

In the 1980s, a cornucopia of alternatives—new financial devices, institutional arrangements, sources of funds—presents itself to the financing of infrastructure improvements. Under the combined stresses of expensive and volatile markets for traditional debt financing, shortages in current revenues, and rapid reversals in federal and state grants, local governments have moved to seek out new ways of packaging and financing needed projects.

The variety of financing options discussed in this chapter not only provide many opportunities; they also illustrate new ways of conducting the public's business combined with new costs and uncertainties. They raise both broad policy and detailed operational questions regarding the desirability of the employment of new techniques—concerns that range from the ability of government to assume greater risks to the implications of complicated legal and financial relationships that may develop in the process of creativity.

Infrastructure improvement—repair, replacement, and new construction—can be financed in a variety of ways. Aside from traditional methods such as the issuance of municipal bonds, numerous innovative methods are available to jurisdictions. Traditionally, a major source of capital funds has been the federal government, but cutbacks at that level have forced innovative financing schemes to be adopted by state and local governments alike. This need has been reinforced because the unfavorable credit conditions that have caused problems for private-sector borrowers also have been at work at the state and local levels.

The catch-all phrase, creative financing, describes a response by governments to uncertian and varying market demands and changing economic factors. These new methods include variable-rate obligations, zero coupon bonds, put option bonds, warrants, and use of third-party guarantees. Short-term borrowing methods not generally associated with capital financing have come into use, such as the issuance of tax-exempt commercial paper and demand and flexible rate notes.

Another way to finance infrastructure projects is to use nondebt sources. Leasing, tax-exempt lease purchase agreements, sale and leaseback of public property to the private sector, and pension fund financing are all being used to maintain, renovate, and rebuild the country's governmental infrastructure.

Public corporations such as self-supporting utilities and off-budget enterprises are gaining more adherents as an alternative means to deliver public services. Both the number and type of these public enterprises have grown in recent years, and although there are critics of this method, the public enterprise concept is generally well accepted by the public and officials alike.

Among a variety of special benefit taxation techniques, tax increment financing is an increasingly popular way to raise revenues for infrastructure purposes. This technique is usually used as the framework for the use of other instruments such as industrial revenue bonds. Although improvement districts are well established in both urban and rural areas, it is just recently that officials have looked upon such districts as economic development tools to provide backing for infrastructure activities.

Finally, public/private partnerships of all shapes, sizes, and varieties are being entered into in order to solve mutual financing problems. To be successful, both sectors of the community must gain from the arrangement. At their best, such arrangements combine the most favorable attributes of both business and government; but the legal structure and negotiations needed to put them in place can be complicated and involve political and economic risks for both parties.

Endnotes

[1] In fact, the occurrence of large operating deficits and cash flow shortages have switched current operating budgets from capital fund providers to demanders of credit, increasing the competition for funds in the market.

[2] Government Finance Research Center, *Resources in Review*, vol. 5, no. 4, July 1983, p. 4.

[3] David P. Allardice, "Small-Issue Industrial Revenue Bonds in the Seventh Federal Reserve District," *Economic Perspectives*, Winter 1982, p. 12.

[4] Ibid., p. 12.

[5] See Petersen and Hough, "Creative."

[6] See Lisa A. Cole, Dawn R. Duven, Samuel H. Owen, and A. John Vogt, *Guide to Municipal Leasing*, (Chicago: Municipal Finance Officers Association), 1983.

[7] Peter Tropper and Anne Kaufman, *Pension Power for Economic Development*, (Washington, DC: Northeast-Midwest Institute), 1980, p. 1.

[8] Industrial Union Department, AFL-CIO *Labor & Investments*, vol. 1, no. 1, January 1981, p. 1.

[9] Tropper and Kaufman, p. 9.

[10] Ibid., p. 9.

[11] Peter F. Drucker, *The Unseen Revolution: How Pension Fund Socialism Came to America*, (New York: Harper and Row), 1976, p. 13.

[12] Lawrence Litvak, *Pension Funds & Economic Renewal*, (Washington, DC: Congressional Budget Office), 1981, p. 3.

[13] Tropper and Kaufman, p. i.

[14] *Labor & Investments*, p. 1.

[15] See Government Finance Research Center, *Public Pension Investment Targeting: A Survey of Practices*, (Washington, DC: Government Finance Research Center), forthcoming.

[16] Tropper and Kaufman, p. 12.

[17] Litvak, pp. 122–123.

[18] Ibid., p. 13.

[19] Ibid., p. 19.

[20] James T. Bennett and Thomas J. DiLorenzo, "The Limitations of Spending Limitation-State and Local Governments: Off-Budget Financing and the Illusion of Fiscal Fitness," *Economic Review*, December 1982, p. 15.

[21] Water Pollution Control Federation, *Sewer Charges for Wastewater Collection and Treatment—A Survey*, (Washington, DC: Water Pollution Control Federation), 1982, pp. 2–4.

[22]Bennett and DiLorenzo, p. 16.

[23]Advisory Commission on Intergovernmental Relations, *Changing Public Attitudes on Government and Taxes*, (Washington, DC: Advisory Commission on Intergovernmental Relations), 1981, p. 7.

[24]Public Securities Association, *Statistical Yearbook of Municipal Finance*, (New York: Public Securities Association), 1981, p. V-7.

[25]U.S. Department of Commerce, *Statistical Abstract of the United States*, (Washington, DC: U.S. Bureau of the Census), 1981, p. 300.

[26]Benjamin Jones, *Tax Increment Financing of Community Redevelopment*, (Lexington, KY: Council of State Governments), 1977, p. 1.

[27]Jonathan M. Davidson, "Tax Increment Financing As a Tool for Community Development," *University of Detroit Journal of Urban Law*, vol. 56, no. 2, Winter 1979, p. 411.

[28]See Michael Newman, "Tax Increment Financing As a Tool for Development and Redevelopment," *The Oregon Law Review*, vol. 61, no. 1, 1982, for a discussion of these issues.

[29]David E. Hartley, "Special Benefit Financing in California," *Resources in Review*, vol. 5, no. 5, September 1983, p. 9.

[30]John M. Gunyou, *Public-Private Partnerships for Economic Development: A Reference Manual for Local Government*, (Denver, CO: Denver Regional Council of Governments), 1982, p. 142.

[31]Ibid., p. 2.

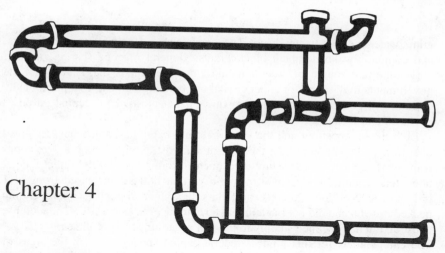

Chapter 4

THE INTERGOVERNMENTAL CONNECTION

This book focuses on the role of state and local governments in providing, financing, and maintaining public infrastructure. However, funding public works and fostering economic development have also been important goals of the federal government, which has been a prominent third partner in public infrastructure investment.

Federal funds and programs provide the catalyst that stimulates much of the capital spending by states and localities; federal capital spending accounts for nearly one-half of all infrastructure expenditures.[1] A brief overview of the nature and extent of federal involvement in public works investment (PWI) illustrates the historic and continuing interdependence of the state-local-federal triangle in the provision of public capital facilities.

Federal Capital Spending

Federal capital spending for infrastructure occurs in two basic forms—direct federal public works investment and intergovernmental assistance. The first category usually includes large scale construction projects such as the building of waterways, dams, reservoirs, and hydroelectric power projects. Intergovernmental assistance frequently is in the form of federal grants-in-aid to state and local governments. These are "categorical" grant programs that provide targeted funds for the acquisition of specific types of physical assets, and broad-based "block" grant programs that provide a flexible source of funding capital projects. Examples of capital intensive grant programs include the Federal Highway Program, water and wastewater disposal programs, urban development action grants, and community development block grants. General revenue sharing, another very important source of federal monies, provides funds that state and local governments may spend for either capital or operating purposes. Approximately one-third of general revenue sharing funds has been used for capital purposes by states and localities.[2]

Both the composition and the size of federal capital spending have changed over time and continue, under the present administration, to form new relationships to state/local infrastructure investment. From 1957 to 1982 direct federal nondefense public works investment (in current dollars) increased from $1.1 billion to $8.5 billion.[3] In constant dollars direct federal public works spending peaked in 1966 and did not reattain that level until 1978. Since 1979, nondefense construction has declined sharply to the real spending levels of the early 1970s.[4] The chief outlets for this kind of federal capital spending are in the areas of natural resources and public buildings construction.

Until recently, federal grants-in-aid have played an increasingly important role in state and local government capital investment. In 1957, federal capital grants-in-aid represented less than one-tenth of the total share of total capital outlays by state and local governments. By 1977, this figure had increased to nearly 40 percent of the total, replacing debt as the largest source of financing public works.[5] In constant 1972 dollars, federal capital grants for public works increased from $12.2 billion in 1957 to $19 billion in 1977.

In certain functional areas, federal grants had become a predominant source of financing. For instance, in 1977, federal grants accounted for 75 percent and 65 percent, respectively, of all state and local capital outlays for sewers and airports. Despite this trend, it should be noted that during this period federal capital grants did not grow as rapidly as total transfers to the states and localities. Whereas capital grants comprised an estimated 35 percent of intergovernmental aid in 1957, by 1977 this figure had declined to slightly over 20 percent.[6]

In the last five years, total federal grants-in-aid have declined as a percentage of federal budget outlays—from an all-time high of 17 percent in 1978 to 11.5 percent in 1982. As seen in Chart 1, 1978 was also the peak year for federal grants as a percentage of state-local budgets. Declining from the 1978 high of 26 percent, federal aid in 1982 contributed slighlty more than 20 percent of state-local expenditures.

In the area of infrastructure assistance, federal grants for public works dropped from a high point of $22.4 billion in 1980 to an estimated $20.2 billion in 1982. But in real (1972) dollar terms, the drop has been much sharper, falling from a peak of $20.8 billion in 1978 to $12.1 billion in 1982.[7]

Impacts of Federal Programs And Policies

Federal policies have impacts beyond the actual construction of public facilities with federal dollars. The availability of federal dollars can cause state and local

CHART 1

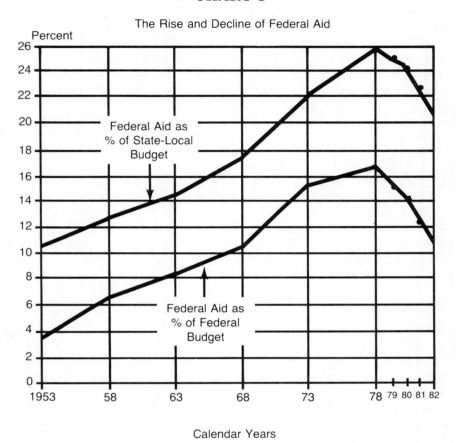

The Rise and Decline of Federal Aid

Calendar Years

SOURCE: John Shannon, "Austerity Federalism—The State-Local Response," in *National Tax Journal*.

governments to shift their priorities regarding capital spending and bias the selection of projects toward those that can obtain federal grants and away from otherwise more attractive projects that are not eligible for grants. Studies by the U.S. General Accounting Office and the American Society of Planning Officials (ASPO) document this federal effect.[8]

Federal standards and requirements also significantly affect the capital budgeting priorities of state and local governments. Stringent water pollution and drinking water standards, detailed noise abatement regulations for airports and highways, air pollution legislation, and federal laws for the handicapped have influenced the capital allocation decisions made by states and localities. Case studies reported by ASPO reveal that even in communities with sound capital budgeting procedures, federal and state mandates often made the selection of certain capital projects a foregone conclusion.

A third major influence is the tendency of federal capital assistance to encourage new construction rather than maintenance and repair of existing capital assets. Federal funding for physical improvements generally prohibits the use of funds for normal maintenance. The presence of funding "carrots" such as 90 percent financing of interstate highway projects and 75 percent matching share of wastewater treatment facilities costs provides strong incentives for state and local officials to choose a program of new construction over an approach that emphasizes ongoing maintenance and repair for which they can expect no federal contribution. Studies by the American Public Works Association, CONSAD, and the Urban Institute document the bias of federal programs against maintenance and the consequent deferral of routine maintenance and repair of existing capital assets by states and localities.[9]

Federal Tax Laws

Thus far, the only federal assistance discussed in relation to state and local infrastructure financing has been that provided through grants and loans. However, another federal initiative—that of tax policy—has become an important element in capital financing approaches of state and local governments. Through tax policy, investors can be attracted to public projects by being able to take advantage of such items as favorable depreciation schedules, the investment tax credit or tax-exempt financing. This section explores recent federal tax laws and how they have influenced investment in public infrastructure.

From a captial markets perspective, a leading—if not the paramount—characteristic of state and local obligations is that the interest income from such debt is exempt from federal taxation (and, frequently, from state and local income taxation as well). This has meant, over the years, that investors seeking shelter from income taxes were willing to pay a premium for these securities, resulting in lower rates of interest that had to be paid by issuers. Typically, state and local borrowers have had to pay rates of interest only 65 to 75 percent of those paid on taxable securities of a similar maturity and credit quality. Recent changes in federal tax policy, however, have served to reduce the value of tax-exemption to states and localities as a means of reducing borrowing costs.

On August 13, 1981, the Economic Recovery Tax Act (ERTA) of 1981 was signed into law, and slightly more than a year later, the Tax Equity and Fiscal Responsibility Act (TEFRA) of 1982 was enacted. Both of these major federal tax reform measures substantially affect efforts by state and local governments to finance public improvements.

Economic Recovery Tax Act of 1981

ERTA instituted sweeping reductions in individual and corporate income taxes, accelerated the depreciation of tangible property, liberalized use of tax-deferred retirement instruments, and authorized new investment instruments.

These changes drastically affect the demand for and costs of tax-exempt municipal securities—the primary source of capital financing utilized by state and local governments. The aggregate of individual income tax reductions wrought by ERTA, along with its minimum tax rate on unearned income, indexing of income tax brackets, and Accelerated Cost Recovery System, serve to reduce significantly the attractiveness of tax-exempt securities among high-income individuals. Such individual investors have played an increasingly important role in recent years in municipal bond markets, currently accounting for nearly one-half of the dollar volume of new municipal bond and note issues.

ERTA created new investment instruments—the Individual Retirement Account (IRA) and the All Savers Certificate—that also have steered investment, particularly from the individual investors, away from the tax-exempt securities market.[10]

Not all provisions of ERTA adversely affected state and local government capital financing. The act allowed tax-exempt financing of vehicles leased for mass commuting and of fire and emergency vehicles, and thus enabled state and local governments to take advantage of some of the creative lease financing techniques described in Chapter 3. The faster depreciation rates available under ERTA have created opportunities for governments to interest the private sector in a variety of sale-leaseback arrangements whereby the governments sell public facilities but continue to operate and use them.

Tax Equity and Fiscal Responsibility Act of 1982[11]

A number of the provisions of the Tax Equity and Fiscal Responsibility Act of 1982 impose substantive and procedural requirements upon the tax-exempt municipal securities markets, adding to the costs and difficulties that confront state and local governments that seek to access this source of capital. Among these are TEFRA's mandates concerning registration of tax-exempt bonds and the subsequent reporting requirements, plus restrictions governing the issuance and use of small issue industrial development bonds (IDBs).[12]

The TEFRA restrictions on the use of industrial development bonds include: (1) a requirement for public approval, (2) a limit on the maturity of IDBs to 120 percent of the reasonable expected economic lives of the facilities financed with the proceeds, (3) a prohibition, in most cases, of the use of the accelerated depreciation schedules created under ERTA on property financed with IDBs, and (4) a limit on their uses to exclude a variety of recreational and commercial uses.

Another major provision of TEFRA that affects the use of debt financing by state and local governments is a limitation on the amount of tax-exempt interest income that can be deducted by banks. This additional cost to banks that hold municipal securities is expected to be passed on to issuers or investors and, thus, diminishes even further the lure of tax-exempt investing.

1983 Tax Actions

The 1983 tax act, whatever its acronym will be, is likely to include a provision to amend ERTA in a way that will significantly diminish the attractiveness of municipal sale-leaseback transactions as well as of traditional operating leases. As a result of legislation introduced in May 1983, units of government may be severely restricted in their ability to sell assets and allow investors to take advantage of various tax benefits that cannot be used by the public sector. Although the characteristics of the final version of this amendment remain to be ironed out, it appears that a longer depreciation schedule will be imposed (on almost all assets whose use is acquired by an operating lease, regardless of whether an asset was previously owned and then sold by a government or whether its use had always been obtained by a lease); and tax-exempt bond financing will not be allowed in conjunction with sale-leasebacks. The major proposal under consideration in the summer of 1983 would make these restrictions effective as of May 23, 1983.

Another item on the 98th Congress' agenda affecting capital facilities financing is additional restrictions on industrial development bond financing. Proposed legislation would curb IDB usage by (1) imposing new limitations on cost recovery for property financed with tax-exempt IDBs, (2) prohibiting the use of tax-exempt IDBs in conjunction with federally insured deposits and (3) limiting small issue IDBs by providing that the bonds be available only to small businesses, that no business have outstanding more than $20 million of small issue bonds at any time and that these bonds not be used to finance land acquisition.

Recent Initiatives in Transportaiton and Public Works

As has been noted, most federal action in the grants-in-aid area has been directed toward cutbacks. Nonetheless, the downturn in the economy, unemployment, and the widely heralded decay of infrastructure did combine to generate some renewal of interest in federal grants for capital purposes.

The Surface Transportation Assistance Act of 1982, which imposed a five-cent per gallon increase in the excise tax on motor fuels and other charges on vehicles and equipment, was dubbed a "highway user fee" by the president. The $5.5 billion in new annual revenues that it is expected to raise will be used to complete construction of the interstate highway system and to undertake rehabilitation of the nation's highways, bridges and mass transit systems. One-fifth of the proceeds from the gas tax revenues are to be allocated for urban transit.

As the bill made its way through the post-election session of the 97th Congress, it enjoyed widespread support from many sectors of the economy for its attempts to address problems of deteriorated public infrastructure. Some state and local government officials, nevertheless, voiced concerns that it would concentrate federal funds, once more, on new construction rather than on maintenance and that the formulas for distributing gas taxes would not target the funds to the most urgent infrastructure problem areas.

In March 1983, Congress, recognizing that "the present condition of the Nation's public facilities threatens national economic recovery, and that job creation, private sector productivity, and local and economic strength is dependent upon public leadership and assistance in rehabilitating, improving, and building essential public facilities," enacted the Emergency Jobs Act of 1983 (PL 98-8). Through this measure, the federal government made $4.6 billion in supplemental FY 83 funds available to units of general local government to be used for construction, renovation, repair, and improvement of local public works. Funds were apportioned among the states on the basis of unemployment rates, with some monies targeted to economically distressed local areas. Definition of public works included a broad range of projects. The act's short-term nature was underscored by its requirement that any funded construction must be completed within a year of receipt of federal funds.

Potential Federal Strategies

What the future role of the federal government concerning public infrastructure development will be is an issue receiving a great deal of attention from Congress, the Administration and, of course, state and local officials. A wide array of proposals have been aired, and some have been the subject of extensive Congressional hearings and public discussion. Prominent among them are:

- A Federal Investment Budget Bill which calls for a federal capital budget, a special analysis of public capital investments, and a nationwide inventory and assessment of public infrastructure facilities.
- A National Development Bank which would provide loans and loan guarantees to finance public works, facilities and economic development projects and which would offer an alternative to the municipal bond market as a source of capital funds.
- A Public Capital Investment Bill that would establish a countercyclical trust fund to be used for state and local government infrastructure grants during periods of high unemployment. One version of this plan would make the establishment of a state infrastructure bank a requirement for participation in the trust fund.
- Enterprise zones would attempt to stimulate private sector development in distressed areas through the use of tax incentives and the relaxation of government regulations.

- A "Rebuilding of America Act" would create a national commission to inventory the nation's public works and develop a ten-year national investments plan.
- In 1982, and again in 1983, the Reagan Administration developed "new federalism" proposals which seek to turn back a number of federal programs to the states. Some of the capital-intensive programs targeted for transfer include mass transit, community development, and federal aid to highways (except the interstate system). Plans call for earmarking of certain existing federal taxes for a new federal trust fund that would belong to the states, which would have much discretion as to how the funds would be spent.

The States' Role

Where do state governments fit into this infrastructure finance picture? State governments have long been associated with both infrastructure and economic development. At times states have played the roles of investor, facilitator and enabler, and regulator in both of these areas. Even though these activities are traditional, the identification and strengthening of the mutually reinforcing linkages between public infrastructure and economic development is a very contemporary concern and a major focus of this book.

The powers of the states are pervasive in matters of allocating the expenditure of public funds, authorizing financing instruments, providing political subdivisions access to particular sources of revenue and capital, and regulating financial institutions and practices. Local governments' ability to initiate, plan, finance, and construct capital facilities derives in great measure from state constitutions, state statutes, and state policies. Therefore, an acknowledgment of the sweeping dimensions of the states' roles in capital resource allocation and recognition of the attendant political and geographic policy considerations are essential steps in any approach to local infrastructure development.

Direct Investment of State Funds

As investors in public facilities, states generally occupy a key position in the provision of such public infrastructure components as highways, roads, bridges, waterways, canals, ports, airports, dams, irrigation projects, water pollution control facilities, water and wastewater treatment plants, schools, prisons, and hospitals.

Total new public construction by all levels of government in the U.S., measured in constant 1977 dollars, has shown a steady decline in recent years, exceeding a seven percent annual rate in 1979 and 1981. Still, the state and local share of that total investment in public facilities continues to hover at 80 percent. The key position of state and local governments as master builder, vis-a-vis the federal government, is demonstrated in Table 5. (The proportion of federal

TABLE 5
Annual Value of New Public Construction Put in Place in the United States: 1978–1982
(In millions of dollars)

Type of construction	Constant (1977) dollars				
	1978	1979	1980	1981	1982
Total public construction	40,816	37,597	37,562	34,898	32,993
State and local construction	33,233	30,809	30,746	28,209	26,539
Total buildings	11,341	10,098	10,634	9,477	8,854
Housing and redevelopment . .	755	850	1,047	1,048	931
Educational	5,549	5,242	5,406	4,343	3,775
Hospital	1,213	917	855	934	839
Other	3,824	3,089	3,326	3,152	3,308
Highways and streets	8,849	8,206	8,180	8,151	8,618
Conservation and development	551	558	615	619	592
Sewer systems	6,146	5,971	5,409	4,163	3,565
Water supply facilities	2,395	2,048	2,456	2,090	1,832
Miscellaneous nonbuilding	3,951	3,928	3,453	3,709	3,077
Federal construction	7,583	6,788	6,815	6,690	6,455
Total buildings	2,209	1,797	1,908	2,040	1,939
Housing	157	79	103	64	117
Industrial	1,058	852	974	1,072	1,048
Educational	20	30	27	19	30
Hospital	417	344	350	415	402
Other	557	491	454	470	341
Highways and streets	366	378	303	290	283
Military facilities	1,331	1,248	1,251	1,271	1,427
Conservation and development	3,553	3,264	3,206	2,995	2,704
Miscellaneous nonbuilding	124	101	148	95	102

SOURCE: Bureau of the Census, U.S. Department of Commerce

construction shrinks even further if spending for military facilities, a function that does not have its state/local counterpart, is removed from the equation.)

Annual reports of state government finances show their expenditures for construction by category. In this series, shown in Table 6, the states' dominance of total public infrastructure spending is demonstrated.

Traditional sources of capital that states tap to directly finance infrastructure and economic development include outlays from the current general fund, "earmarked revenues" and enterprise funds, short- and long-term debt, and federal grants-in-aid. States are more and more frequently authorizing creative financing

TABLE 6
Summary of State Government Direct Expenditure Capital Outlay for Construction: 1980, 1981, 1982
(In millions of dollars)

Purpose and function	1980	1981	1982
Total.........................	19.736	20.632	19.560
General expenditure	19.067	19.800	18.718
Education services:			
Education........................	2.127	2.574	2.644
Institutions of higher education	1.525	1.919	2.148
Local schools...................	293	336	315
Other	309	318	182
Libraries........................	3	8	5
Social services:			
Public welfare	29	23	36
Vendor payments for medical care..	—	—	—
Cash assistance payments.........	—	—	—
Other vendor payments..........	—	—	—
Other	29	23	36
Hospitals	720	721	765
State hospitals	577	629	760
Other	143	92	5
Health..........................	266	373	257
Employment Security Administration..	11	8	4
Veterans services.................	1	1	2
Transportation:			
Highways.......................	13,526	13,269	12,121
Toll highways	461	448	412
Regular highway facilities	13,065	12,820	11,709
Airports	220	146	159
Water transport and terminals........	156	241	254
Public safety:			
Police protection	31	29	26
Correction	490	527	569
Protective inspection and regulation,			
N.E.C.......................	2	2	5
Environment and housing:			
Natural resources.................	282	327	432
Housing and urban renewal	57	67	45
Sewerage	242	217	233
Parks and recreation	255	304	257
Governmental administration:			
Financial administration	14	9	20
General control	32	19	46
General public buildings...........	295	359	363
Interest on debt	—	—	—
Miscellaneous commercial activities	16	14	3
All other.........................	289	562	472
Insurance trust expenditure.............	—	—	—
Liquor stores expenditure	1	1	3
Utilities expenditure	669	832	840

Note: Because of reounding, detail may not add to total.
— Represents zero or rounds to zero.
SOURCE: Bureau of the Census, *State Government Finances in 1980, 1981*, and unpublished data.

instruments of the types described in Chapter 3 in attempts to increase their capital resources. Another strategy that states employ is the use of public funds to leverage greater private sector investment in economic development projects with public infrastructure components.

States also share in the financing of local infrastructure with their local political subdivisions by providing funds via state aid, or revenue sharing programs, and from federal funds "passed through" by the state to the local government. State aid has historically been an important source of local government revenues, especially in the functional areas of education and transportation, and has sometimes served to finance local capital expenditures. Local water pollution control facilities backed by a combination of state and federal funds provide a good example of this type of activity.

During the early 1970s, federal pass-through funds became an increasingly important source of capital financing for local governments, particularly for the construction of wastewater treatment plants, hospitals and health facilities, mass transportation systems and urban renewal projects.[13]

As the federal government in the early 1980s relinquished some of its previous role in water pollution control financing, many states re-evaluated their commitment to these projects and programs. At the same time, state participation through grants and loans increased. A 1982 survey of state activities in such programs shows that a majority—27 states—provide grants to help local governments finance their share of the costs for projects funded through the federal construction grants program. Most states that have grant programs contribute between 10 and 15 percent of the project costs. State loan programs help to finance local government water pollution control facilities in 13 states. Loans that are available in those states help localities to fund 25 percent of project costs.[14]

The State as Intermediary

For the ability to raise funds, incur debt, and control the allocation of resources, local governments depend upon the powers granted to them by the state. A state-mandated tax limitation measure such as Proposition 13 in California or Proposition 2-1/2 in Massachusetts, for example, may limit the amount of revenues a city can collect through its property tax. State law also determines whether or not the city may impose a local sales, income, or excise tax. If local officials wish to borrow money to finance capital construction, it is the state that authorizes or restricts the use of particular debt instruments such as general obligation bonds, municipal revenue bonds, and industrial development bonds, to name a few. In many states debt limitations, interest rate limits, and other controls place a variety of constraints on the nature and extent of borrowing by local government.[15] Clearly, access to capital by local governments for the purpose of building streets, sewer mains, fire stations, or for fostering economic development, is shaped by numerous forces beyond the local tax base and local economic and political conditions.

By their legislative activities state governments frequently act as facilitators in order to expand the range of tools available to local officials for both infrastructure and economic development. Typical forms of state enabling legislation involve industrial development bonds, independent authorities or commissions with revenue-raising and/or debt incurring powers, provisions for the establishment of special assessment districts, tax increment financing, and other mechanisms. The users of these and other financing vehicles and institutional arrangements were described in chapter three; the focus here is to emphasize the degree to which local governments' access to such tools is dependent upon state actions.

Another state approach has concentrated on assistance to local governments in the design and implementation of economic development strategies. These efforts have generally taken the form of state industrial or economic development commissions, and statewide urban strategies.

An extensive research project conducted by Charles R. Warren of the National Academy of Public Administration, published in 1980, analyzed this type of state activity from detailed case studies of 10 states.[16] Warren found four common major themes in the urban strategies of those states:

- an economic development theme with an emphasis on job creation and retention, industrial development, and business attraction/expansion;
- a growth management component;
- urban revitalization policies primarily concerned with increased housing supply and improved public facilities and services; and
- a fiscal reform emphasis in the areas of improving local tax system equity and the fiscal capacity of local governments.

Providing incentives for attracting business and industry, a third facilitiating activity of state governments, opens up avenues by which both local and state governments pursue private sector investments. Traditionally, these incentives have provided for property tax abatements of various kinds, a wide range of corporate income tax exemptions, and other special tax credits or exemptions extended to industry. Other incentive programs have focused on the provision of free land or industrial plant sites for industry and assistance to local governments with related public works projects.

Incentives made available by states frequently take the form of financial assistance to industry. Loans or loan guarantees for industrial construction, aid for existing plant expansions, and job training assistance are common examples.[17]

A report prepared for the National Governors' Association in 1983 provides a state-by-state chart of capital financing and economic development incentives. It also describes a host of generic incentives that states have initiated or participate in. This compendium includes:

- community development corporations,
- community development loan guarantees,
- development companies,

- direct loan programs and revolving loan funds,
- guaranteed or insured loans,
- industrial revenue bonds,
- job development authorities,
- linked deposit plans,
- pollution control financing guarantee programs,
- product development corporations,
- public pension fund investments,
- secondary market support,
- small business investment companies,
- small business loans,
- land banking and industrial parks,
- tax-exempt bonds and bond packaging,
- tax increment financing, and
- venture capital companies.[18]

In recent years states have developed innovative programs to make capital more readily available to local governments as a source of funding for economic development and infrastructure investment. Recent innovations such as bond banks, development loan funds, public utilities financing banks, and proposed infrastructure development banks are discussed in the following sections.

Bond Banking

In 1969, Vermont was the first state to institute a bond bank to help local governments gain access to credit markets that would otherwise not be available to them. By pooling their needs for capital into one large debt offering and then marketing it through the state bond bank, smaller jurisdictions in the state were able to employ more long-term financing at more favorable interest rates than they could have expected as the sole issuer of bonds.

Maine, New Hampshire, and Alaska now operate similar bond banking institutions. New York has established the structure for operating a bond bank, but by mid-1983 it was not yet active. The Maine Bond Bank, perhaps the most active, has outstanding debt of $217 million. In operation for 10 years and having issued bonds on behalf of 370 municipal corporations in the state, it usually goes to market twice a year with an issue of approximately $15 million.

Development Loan Programs

Development loan programs in a number of states provide funds at below-market interest rates for the finance of industrial plant construction, expansion, or equipment. Loans are made available to enterprises either directly or via state or local industrial development authorities. Program funding is often provided from state tax revenues. Typically, a one-time start-up grant provides an initial sum of money which becomes a revolving fund as loans are made and repaid.

Kentucky has drawn capital for development loans from its pension funds; Alaska has used its oil lease royalties and severance taxes; New York and Minnesota have used federal funds from the Economic Development Administration; and others have issued bonds.

In *Innovations in Development Finance* (1979) Lawrence Litvak and Belden Daniels examine the range of approaches states have used to assist businesses in amassing capital. Summarizing their discussion of direct loan programs, they conclude that the experience is extremely mixed.

> Their lack of need to adhere to strict market sensitivity gives them the potential to undertake substantial risk. Most direct loan programs have responded to that opportunity either by being far more conservative than they need be, or far less financially sound than they ought to have been.[19]

The New Jersey Infrastructure Development Bank

A proposal for establishing a state infrastructure development bank, under consideration by the State of New Jersey, attracted widespread attention in 1983. The intent of this financing mechanism is to amass a pool of capital that would be made available to New Jersey's local governments. This would be done through grants and loans, made at reduced rates and on terms more favorable than otherwise available. The bank, a revolving loan fund intended to be a self-supporting operation, would be empowered to make loans to governmental units to finance specified capital improvements or property acquisitions. The infra-structure bank would also serve as a statewide financing vehicle for the local share of projects costs, as well as the vehicle through which the state itself could issue revenue-backed bonds for various infrastructure purposes. A variety of methods of capitalizing the bank have been proposed, most of which combine federal funds with state appropriations, the proceeds of state bond issues, revenues, and possibly private capital.

In California, Massachusetts, and Minnesota similar proposals were under consideration late in 1983.

The Maine Public Utilities Financing Bank

Under legislation enacted in 1981, Maine established a Public Utilities Financing Bank to provide capital to private corporations for building public utility facilities. Projects that deal with water, electricity, gas, energy conservation measures, and renewable energy resources may be funded at reduced interest by the bank. It will primarily service small, rural areas and will concentrate on new construction. The state had completed the structuring of the bank, which will raise capital by selling its own bonds and notes on the municipal bond market, but by mid-1983 the bank had not yet begun to place loans.

The Regulatory Role of the State

The availability of capital for infrastructure and economic development is greatly influenced by the regulatory powers that states wield over financial institutions. Even though regulation of the bond market is a federal prerogative, the oversight of financial institutions such as insurance companies and state public pension funds falls to the states. The activities of commercial banks and savings and loan institutions come under the aegis of both the federal and state regulators.

The regulation of financial institutions is primarily concerned with: the creation, operation, and expansion of financial markets; the liabilities of the institutions; and the uses of their assets. The latter is a matter of importance with respect to targeting investments toward specific public goals—be they local economic development, infrastructure finance, or other objectives.

Usury laws, or interest rate limitations, is another province of state regulation that can have an impact on the ability of both the private and public sectors to borrow funds. This was demonstrated in the early 1980s when interest rates rose to historically high levels. Some states found themselves shut out of the municipal bond market due to usury laws that had been established by the state in an era of less costly borrowing. Legislation was enacted by some states to restore access to this source of capital by governmental units.

Summary

A review of trends in federal participation in infrastructure financing has shown capital spending on the decline as a proportion of total federal outlays. Nevertheless, the contributions and impacts made by direct federal public works investment and grants are substantial. Not only does federal spending account for more than half of all investments in the nation's public capital stock, it exerts a strong influence on the selection and priority setting of state and local capital investment projects. The lack of federal aid for most kinds of maintenance instills bias toward new construction, often at the expense of caring for the existing network of roads and water and sewer systems.

Revisions to the federal tax laws in 1981 and 1982 reduced the attractiveness of municipal bonds as an investment vehicle and imposed many restrictions governing the use of this main source of financing capital projects by state and local governments. Attempts to restrict tax-exempt financing mechanisms continued in 1983 with much attention focused on sale-leaseback transactions.

In 1983 a plethora of proposals that would alter the federal role in infrastructure investment vied for the attention of Congress. Some would increase the level of federal investment for public facilities, some would change the way in which the federal government treats capital spending, and others would shift the funding of capital intensive programs to the states and increase the role of the private sector in public infrastructure investment.

Despite the strong federal influence, the states continue to occupy a key position in building prosperity, exercising far reaching and diverse powers in infrastructure finance and economic development. The extensive reach of state powers adds political and geographic dimensions to policy decisions concerned with the planning of both urban and rural development. Some of the specific financial practices used by states plus a number of diverse methods of funding local projects point to the different roles played by state governments. States act as investors, intermediaries, and regulators in this process and, thus, have a stake in both the financing of public infrastructure projects that are too costly or beyond the scope of local governments, and the pursuit of economic development that will benefit not just the locality in which the project takes place but the state as a whole.

Endnotes

[1]CONSAD, Executive Summary, p. 22.

[2]CONSAD, Final Report, p. 3.88.

[3]U.S. Office of Management and Budget, "Federal Outlays for Major Physical Capital Investment, (Washington, DC: unpublished) 1983, p. 4.

[4]Ibid., p. 5.

[5]Ibid.

[6]Nazir G. Dossani and Wilber A. Steger, "Trends in U.S. Public Works Investment: Report on a New Study," *National Tax Journal*, vol. 33, no. 2; June 1980, p. 134.

[7]U.S. Office of Management and Budget, "Federal Outlays," p. 5.

[8]Comptroller General of the U.S. "Effective Planning," p. 25 and, American Society of Planning Officals, "Local Capital," p. 3.

[9]See Peterson et al, *Stock*.

[10]John E. Petersen, "An Analysis of the Impact of the All Savers Certificate Plan on the Municipal Securities Market," (Washington, DC: Government Finance Research Center), 1981, p. ii.

[11]Adapted from John C. Bates, Jr. and Robert W. Doty, *The Impact of 1982 Federal Legislation on Tax-Exempt Financing*, (New York: Sorg Printing Co.), 1982.

[12]John E. Petersen, "Municipal Bonds in Registered Form," *Resources in Review*, November 1982, vol. 4, no. 6, pp. 6–9.

[13]See Seymour Sacks and Albert J. Richter, *Recent Trends in Federal and State Aid to Local Governments*, (Washington, DC: U.S. Advisory Commission on Intergovernmental Relations), 1980.

[14]Government Finance Research Center, *Financing Water Pollution Control: The State Role* (Washington, DC: Environmental Protection Agency), 1982, pp. 17–27.

[15]See John E. Petersen, Lisa A. Cole, and Maria L. Petrillo, *Watching and Counting: A Survey of State Assistance to and Supervision of Local Debt and Financial Administration*, (Chicago: Municipal Finance Officers Association), 1977.

[16]See Charles R. Warren, *The States and Urban Strategies: A Comparative Analysis*, (Washington, DC: U.S. Department of Housing and Urban Development), 1980.

[17]See Roger J. Vaughan, *Rebuilding America, vol. 1*, (Washington, DC: The Council of State Planning Agencies), 1983.

[18]Chemical Bank, *Guide to State Capital Formation Incentives and Innovations, Second Edition*, (Washington, DC: National Governors' Association), 1983, p. iv.

[19]Lawrence Litvak and Belden Daniels, *Innovations in Development Finance, (Washington, DC: Council of State Planning Agencies), 1979, p. 110.*

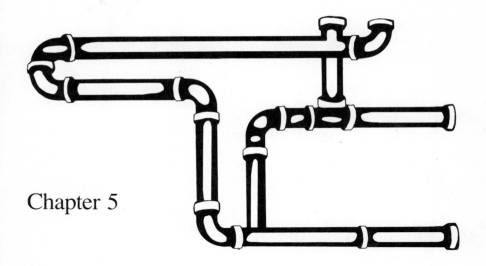

Chapter 5

THE FUTURE CONNECTION

As discussed in the preceeding chapters, the magnitude of the investment backlog and the resources required to maintain existing infrastructure remain a matter of debate. Regardless of how large the infrastructure problem is in the aggregate, government officials individually face tough choices in allocating funds for capital projects. Capital and operating budget decisions made by local governments, principally, determine the type and quality of infrastructure found in the cities and towns of this country. The multitude of resource allocation methods used by local governments, therefore, assumes critical importance in determining the future of the nation's public works.

Federal legislation and regulatory policy cannot be overlooked either, since federal law mandates certain infrastructure programs such as wastewater treatment. In other instances, federal laws affect regional patterns of economic development through interstate highway and waterway projects. These federal programs often require collateral state or local financing, which, in turn, complicates funding priorities and affects the fiscal health of local governments. State-sponsored initiatives and requirements exert similar pressures on local governments' capacity to plan and finance public facilities.

As project financing is intimately connected with project selection, traditional and creative capital financing alternatives add another level of complexity to capital allocation decisions. Coordination of public infrastructure planning with private sector development through public/private joint ventures is yet another dimension of the challenge. Again, the intergovernmental aspect is important, perhaps critical, because of influences that tax and regulatory policies have on the cost and effectiveness of public/private financial relationships.

"The relationship between infrastructure and economic development is an almost hopelessly enormous issue," advises Pamela Plumb, City Councilwoman of Portland, Maine.[1] Although some strides have been made in identifying the gaps in our knowledge regarding the relationship between infrastructure and development, there exists no definitive findings that lay the foundations for policy prescriptions. Rather, progress appears to be most possible in incrementally strengthening the often weak or nonexistent relationship between physical planning, economic development, and financial planning. Bromides aside, realistic development and infrastructure policies that are to be financed by a jurisdiction's own resources need to be designed side-by-side, because the future need for facilities will generally dictate their affordability as well. Like it or not, capital planning puts everybody in the forecasting business.

The attention-getting and national policy-setting discussions dwell on the aggregate and seek global generalizations. This should not becloud the fact that solutions will be achieved on a case-by-case, project-by-project basis. The future connection revolves around the extent to which past lessons are learned, best practice is identified and transferred, and service-providing responsibilities are better matched with financial resources in providing for tomorrow's infrastructure needs.

How Large Is the Problem?

While there is unanimous agreement that the nation's public works are in trouble, no one agrees upon a benchmark to measure the severity of the infrastructure problem. Inundated by vivid and sometimes disastrous examples of infrastructure failures reported by the media, researchers have attempted to establish the magnitude of the infrastructure crisis.[2] Estimates of the level of infrastructure investment required to maintain existing levels of service range from $500 billion to $3 trillion.[3] The great variation in these estimates is due to researchers' assumptions about what constitutes infrastructure, the condition of existing facilities, and their judgments concerning acceptable levels of service, rather than to inaccuracies or miscalculation of data.[4]

Assumptions also shape local governments' perceptions of their individual infrastructure needs. For example: if a water system is 60 years old and its useful life has been assumed to be 50 years, the cost of replacing that system would be considered part of a city's cost of maintaining existing levels of service. On the other hand, if the useful life is assumed to be 80 years, estimates of the investment backlog through the end of the century would be reduced.

The development of performance standards for public facilities could be one of the major benefits that result from the implementation of a comprehensive inventory of public works at the local level. It might also dislodge some commonly held misconceptions about infrastructure problems. Press accounts of infrastructure failure sometimes infer that the age of a facility is the sole measure of its service life.[5] Some very old components, however, provide good service while some newer components must frequently be replaced.[6] So age alone is not a good gauge of the condition of the infrastructure; it should be used in conjunction with information about usage and environment, ranging from traffic conditions to soil composition.[7] Service lives of identical equipment may therefore vary depending on location. This information can be incorporated in a thorough assessment of infrastructure condition to influence the maintenance and replacement priorities of local governments.

A comprehensive inventory may be desirable; its practicality is another matter.

Inventorying Public Facilities

The major challenge to the implementation of an inventory system is how to make sure that the information can be used by both the operating agencies responsible for specific facilities and by the budget specialists who are responsible for resource allocation decisions.

A limited survey of local governments conducted by the Urban Institute regarding infrastructure maintenance practices revealed the following kinds of information typically being collected by state and local governments:

- engineering indicators such as pipe capacity loss or infiltration rates, for water and sewer systems, and skid resistance and loss of original surface for streets;
- intermediate performance ratings such as number of bus and subway car breakdowns for transit systems, pipe breaks for water and sewer systems;
- service-impact indicators such as additional wear on vehicles due to poor street surfaces, number of citizen complaints related to all types of capital assets, number of basement floodings due to poor storm drainage systems; and
- unit costs as indicators that the efficiency of a capital asset may be declining and that some further attention is warranted.[8]

The highly decentralized nature of local government resource allocation implies that the institutional obstacles standing between the theory and the practical application of inventory systems are formidable ones. The Urban Institute concluded from its survey of procedures used to assess infrastructure that although the best of current practices are adequate, regular assessment of infrastructure is rarely practiced by local governments. The type and quality of information collected varies among cities as well as among operating agencies in the same city.

Even though local officials who are directly involved in maintaining facilities tend to believe that they have an adequate grasp of the maintenance needs of the systems they monitor, their information is seldom conveyed in a detailed or systematic way to those who analyze operating and capital budget priorities.[9] At the same time, central budget or planning offices give operating agencies little if any guidance in how to collect information that would help them to establish priorities for project funding.[10]

The absence of a formalized information-gathering and dissemination system hinders efforts to employ such data in the evaluation of maintenance strategies and options, as well as in the effort to define more accurately the infrastructure problems. Local officials do perceive the need for improvements. According to the Urban Institute study: "None of the personnel in the local governments we contacted were anywhere near satisfied with their processes and the information forthcoming from them. And these views were from governments identified as among the 'forerunners' in capital infrastructure planning!"[11]

In conjunction with the Rand Corporation, Aaron Gurwitz and G. Thomas Kingsley produced a detailed system to gather and analyze information for the purpose of formulating economic development policy in the Cleveland metropolitan area.[12] Their system analyzes demographic and socioeconomic trends in concert with performance indicators of specific industries. A similar system might be applied to infrastructure issues. The Rand analysis emphasizes the uniqueness of each city and regional economy and stresses the need for each jurisdiction to develop an economic strategy suited to its particular situation. The creation of an extensive information system, part of that economic strategy, is based on their premise that the more knowledge is available to permit comparisons of costs and benefits among different types of projects, the more strategic thinking will be facilitated.[13]

Successful implementation of an information and strategic planning system like the one developed by Gurwitz and Kingsley requires the commitment of local government staff not only to use but continuously to update the system in their daily activities. The quality and the usefulness of the data can be enhanced when staff members see the information actively incorporated into the planning processes they use. Based on its studies of capital improvement decisions, the Urban Institute suggests that it is prudent to implement such systems on an incremental basis. It notes that many information systems have run into problems because of an overly ambitious application of systems principles.[14] The Government Finance Research Center found this same concern prominent among city financial managers who participated in an on-site technical assistance program in 1980 which helped the City of Cleveland to develop a financial management information system.[15]

The foregoing discussion illustrates that the severity of an "infrastructure crisis" will depend upon the replacement and maintenance standards used by a jurisdiction. In this, the quality of the available information is of critical importance. An inventory of capital facilities and their condition is a basic tool for use in the allocation of capital and operating budget revenues. But, it is only a tool and not a solution in and of itself.

The object of an inventory is not to gauge past deficiencies or, for that matter, even present shortcomings. The basis by which to judge adequacy when it comes to repair, replacement, or expansion should be what will be needed in the future to sustain acceptable levels of service at affordable tax rates and user charges. By definition, capital investments have multi-year service lives and will be used by passing parades of users that, directly or indirectly, will benefit by them and should contribute to their operation, upkeep, and replacement. The planning, both physical and financial, should be performed in the context of what the future users will need and be able to afford. Such planning—identifying future feasible goals and devising means of achieving them—comes under the popular heading of "strategic planning."

Strategic Planning and Government Budgets

In government the linkage between planning and doing is the budget. Capital and operating budgets ultimately give substance to the infrastructure maintenance and development policies of local governments. But, are those policies clearly ennunciated, internally consistent, and mutually supportive? Furthermore, is there a strategy for their accomplishment? Without a strategy, without clearly defined goals and accurate information, resource allocation decisions with long-term consequences may be haphazard, inconsistent, and be swayed by short-term considerations.

Strategic planning embodies a future orientation, a willingness to analyze risk and uncertainty, an ability to compare existing resources with projected future needs, and a clearly stated policy concerning goals and objectives.[16] Ironically, as traditional forms of public sector planning have declined in popularity, planning methods developed for private firms have been proposed as a way to improve the capital and operating budget process.[17] Advocates of this view state that if strategic planning is to be successful, local governments will be well advised to modify their organizational structure to accommodate this new approach.[18] Those whose main interests lie in the area of local government budgeting also see the need to change current budgetary practices.[19] However, budget professionals have not been quick to embrace the new techniques being discussed.

Local government budgeting was created at the beginning of this century as a way to concentrate financial authority in the executive branch of government.[20] The predominant form of budget preparation, commodity-based or line-item budgeting, enumerates items to be purchased such as labor (salaries) and physical assets (inventory and equipment). The line-item framework emphasizes analysis of incremental changes in cost over time. Such analysis is relatively easy to perform, given the time constraints of the annual budget process. Typically, attention is devoted to the most significant changes from the preceding year's budget, since all expenditures cannot be reviewed with the same degree of thoroughness. The funding from the previous year, the base budget, is not analyzed on a cost-benefit basis; the increment, rather than the program, is evaluated.

Budgeting that uses incremental analysis and a commodity format does not lend itself to fundamental changes in program design.[21] The commodity-oriented format tends to produce changes in expenditure patterns that are unrelated to service levels because objects that are purchased and not program accomplishments are the basis for spending decisions. A continued emphasis on the cost of commodities has fostered a preoccupation with budgetary methods to control expenditures rather than to cost programs. Accordingly, budget officials who seek to avoid cost overruns and to squirrel away some funds for an emergency incorporate administrative controls to keep program managers within their budgets.[22]

Reviews of planning techniques suggest that strategic planning needs are often overlooked when capital projects are put in the budget. Strategic planning is not significantly different from the ideal goals outlined for the capital improvement planning process described in Chapter 2. Public sector managers, however, tend to overlook the connection between such planning and capital allocation decisions. They may see the planning document as simply a wish list for professional planners, say those who have studied strategic planning.[23]

Existing practice is not a reliable guide to future performance, and one should not assert that strategic planning cannot successfully be incorporated into budgeting because of political considerations. Developments such as increasing competition in the world economy, continued difficulties for borrowers relying on the tax-exempt bond market, and the withdrawal of federal assistance may force local governments to restructure their existing methods of allocating resources. Clearly, to the extent that local governments must increasingly fend for themselves in planning and paying for improvements (and do so in an environment of intense competition with other jurisdictions for jobs and wealth), the more "market-sensitive" and "business-like" practice are likely to evolve.

For many jurisdictions, planning is already strategic in its scope and character. Norfolk, Virginia; Dayton, Ohio; St. Paul, Minnesota; and Dallas, Texas, have begun to take strategic planning into account as their budgets are developed. They all look at the demands on the operating budget that might be caused by capital expenditures. They also plan maintenance strategies for existing facilities based on sophisticated systems developed specifically for that purpose.[23] Although an analysis of innovative local government budget practices is beyond the scope of this volume, it can be stated that such practices have begun to attract widespread attention among practitioners.

A particularly impressive example of physical and financial planning combined into a cohesive strategy is the Urban Services Policy of the City of Portland, Oregon.[24] Like many cities, Portland is severely restricted in its ability to expand its boundaries by Oregon's annexation statutes that require voter approval of the area to be annexed. Consequently, most of Portland's territorial expansions have been limited to small piecemeal additions, largely initiated by the property owners rather than the city.

To create a positive climate toward annexation the city developed an Urban Services Policy, which explicitly states the city's intentions to expand various municipal services—police, fire, sewers, parks, and planning—into the unincorporated areas. More than 150,000 persons currently live in the highly urbanized areas that lie adjacent to but outside, incorporated cities. Much of the unincorporated territory lacks sufficient municipal services. In particular, the lack of sanitary sewers has been identified as both a potential health problem and an impediment to economic development.

The city conducted several studies to identify key policy and financial issues, and to clarify Portland's appropriate role in providing municipal services to the unincorporated areas located adjacent to the city. The studies concluded that: (1) the present lack of services in the unincorporated area constrains the region's economic growth and may create long-term health hazards; (2) most of the region's future industrial sites are located in the unincorporated area, but currently lack basic municipal services; (3) the city has the physical, financial, and institutional capacity to serve a wider area; and (4) the city must know where it will ultimately be responsible for providing services in order to efficiently plan, design, and construct facilties to serve both existing and future services areas. After several drafts and public hearings, the city council adopted the comprehensive Urban Services Policy which establishes a consistent framework for city actions regarding municipal services within the urbanized, unincorporated territory surrounding it. It is a formal declaration by the city that it will address service deficiencies in the nearby unincorporated areas.

To implement the Policy, Portland took several substantive steps that have required the commitment and cooperation of city agencies, the political leaders and staff of other jurisdictions, community groups, and the public, it:

(1) amended the city's comprehensive land use plan;

(2) entered into formal negotiations with the surrounding jurisdictions to jointly determine the Portland urban services boundary;

(3) negotiated interim and wholesale service agreements with existing service providers operating within the boundary; and

(4) esbablished a formal process to promote public awareness and citizen participation in the implementation of the strategy.

Thus, the City of Portland has undertaken an aggressive stance in establishing its commitment to being the urban services provider to the region. It has many things going for it and has established those as positive initiatives in enhancing its economic position in the area.

Federal Policy: Help or Hindrance?

Strong reactions stem from discussions of the role of the federal government in infrastructure development. Some experts think that the federal influence has greatly contributed to the problems that are now being faced by local governments. Poor coordination among federal programs, sometimes overwhelming program requirements, and a lack of a federal capital budget have fostered a reactive style of capital facilities planning and maintenance by local governments.[25]

Federal programs have shown a potential to encourage local governments to fund projects in excess of their revenue-raising ability. They finance construction costs but place the burden of future maintenance on the local government.[26] Historically, few federal grants have been available for maintaining capital projects.[27] Some federal programs, such as those administered by the Urban Mass Transit Administration, reflect the federal bias for new construction; replacement of rolling stock is favored over continued maintenance.[28] The Congressional Budget Office's study of public works, however, indicates that the lack of federal concern about maintenance expenditures may be changing.[29]

The short time horizon for the federal government's appropriations exacerbates the problems of coordinating local, state, and federal infrastructure expenditures.[30] Legislation proposing a federal capital budget may prove to be one method of addressing these issues.[31]

Federal infrastructure programs have altered the physical characteristics and economic potential of state and local governments. They are thought to have played a role in stimulating shifts in employment to the southern and western regions of the nation.[32] Evidence also suggests that suburban and rural areas have benefited more from federal infrastructure expenditures than the central cities.[33]

Also, local governments tend to shift their capital priorities in response to the "carrot and stick" system of federal program requirements, thus deemphasizing their own needs.[34] The capital project rating systems of certain local governments favor projects financed entirely or in part through federal appropriations.[35]

But not all the winds blowing from Washington have been ill when it comes to public works. Aside from the huge dollar sums that have been transfered for state and local use, other benefits for all state and local governments have also flowed from the federal involvement in infrastructure development. Grant requirements have motivated state and local governments to collect information regularly on bridge and wastewater treatment facility conditions.[36] Federal procedures have also served as models for many local governments that have designed their own condition assessment systems. The federal emphasis on standardization of reporting practices and thoroughness has improved the quality of information that is available to local governments. Vagueness and subjectivity in the evaluation of individual facilities are major problems with the data that are currently being gathered.[37]

The project selection process and financing decisions always have been interrelated. But since so much of the life-cycle costs of improvements will be absorbed locally, local governments are increasingly evaluating maintenance strategies and project proposals on their own merits, rather than instigating projects on the basis of the availability of certian types of financing—be they federal grants, state aid, or other sources of funding. Given the uncertainties of the tax-exempt bond market and reductions in federal financing for a wide range of programs, local governments have responded by seeking new means of securing financing. There are several tiers of options that governments can explore.

First, one of the oldest methods for increasing local government access to the capital markets is the design of new financial instruments to stimulate demand for tax-exempt securities. (Traditional financing instruments as well as many of the recent innovative mechanisms were discussed in detail in Chapter 3.)

A frequent outcome of the effort to develop new instruments and entries to the financial markets is the need for new financing vehicles to accommodate their use. A leading example of this type of interaction between "new issues" and "new issuers" has been the growth in enterprise debt, secured on non-tax sources, and the corresponding growth in special funds, authorities, and districts to accommodate their use. This mutual development has been further sped along by the adoption by governments of new public purposes (such as the provision of housing, job opportunties, health care) that have not traditionally come within the ambit of local government concerns.

A second strategy of local governments for coping with fiscal stringency and expanded responsibilities consists of shifting the burden of infrastructure development to the private sector in the form of connection fees, exactions, and systems development charges. This option appears to have been most successful in areas where market forces have stimulated demand for housing or commercial and industrial services. Localities attempting to stimulate development in deteriorated areas sometimes experience difficulties in shifting the cost of infrastructure development to the private sector and, instead, must rely on targeted tax abatements and regulatory relief to attract the private sector to these areas.[38]

Akin to the greater application of the special district/user-charge approach is a third alternative: transferring the responsibility for the provision of a service and/or ownership of a facility to the private sector. "Privatization" of an activity can have many motivations, and a leading one has been to facilitate the renewal or acquisition of capital facilities. Changes in the federal tax code that made possible the passing on of considerable tax advantages to private investors appeared to open up many areas of the use of privatization as a means of financing certain public facilities at lower costs to state and local governments than through conventional means. However, concerns over the loss of federal revenues as a result of potentially widespread use of privatization of public capital led to the introduction of legislation that, if successful, will squelch the capital financing incentives.

A fourth avenue of strategy focuses on transferring more of the load of financing to the state level. The states can assist localities in a wide variety of ways in addressing their infrastructure needs. Virtually every technique has been employed, ranging from technical assistance, loans, grants to localities, all the way through the state taking on responsibility for the service. As in the case of local strategizing, the political and financial situations of each state needs to be examined individually to determine which arrangements are feasible under the circumstances. Nonetheless, the greater popular interest in infrastructure financing may be expanding the horizons of what is doable by the states. State referenda on infrastructure bond issues decided as this book goes to press did surprisingly well around the country, reversing a trend of voter rejection.[39] Evidently, the public in many states were convinced that investments in public works were worthwhile, a necessary ingredient in ensuring their cities' (and their own) future livelihoods.

The connections between infrastructure and economic development are often cited as the major motivation for finding solutions to the "infrastructure crisis."

Infrastructure, Economic Development, and Jobs

The economic significance of the infrastructure-economic development connection is based on common-sense observations:

- the development of the basic transportation system enables previously inaccessible areas to offer private industry competitively priced transportation access to goods and supply markets;
- sewer and water systems are needed to complement the transportation network; and
- residential construction triggers the need for additional infrastructure in the form of health, educational, and recreational facilities.

As flawless as the deductive reasoning might appear, there is no consensus about the significance of infrastructure's impact on business location decisions. Much of the literature and discussion about the importance of infrastructure implicitly assumes that infrastructure development policies will result in an increased level of economic activity. The problem appears to be that while a certain level of infrastructure development is a necessary prerequisite, it is not a sufficient condition to guarantee that development will occur. While discussions about business location decisions are not directly concerned with the infrastructure needs and financing they can provide insights into evaluating the economic significance of infrastructure facilities.

Roger Schmenner's analysis of business location decisions provides evidence that *Fortune 500* companies take advantage of infrastructure assistance more than any other type of assistance.[40] However, he concludes that use of these incentives will vary among firms according to size and the nature of the new facility. As Table 7 shows, government assistance of an infrastructure-related variety is frequently a factor in the location of new plant openings: 38 percent of the firms in the case of roads, sewers, water; 10 percent in the case of sewerage treatment; and 6 percent in the case of traffic and parking. In the case of where the new facility is a relocation rather than an expansion of facilities (a mover plant), all governmental assistance seems less important (except for tax concessions).

Schmenner's work on the business location decisions of smaller firms revealed that the migration patterns of small firms differ from those of their larger counterparts, as do their motivations for moving. Plants that relocate near their original site are typically smaller than plants that move long distances. Moreover, plants that move short distances show a tendency to lease their production space, while those that move further away tend to own their production space. Smaller firms tend to expand and contract more rapidly than large firms, and they move in order to alleviate crowding, as is demonstrated by David Birch's work on small business.[41]

In contrast, large firms are more conscious of cost reduction factors. They are more likely to alter their production processes dramatically in conjunction with a move, which frequently lowers the labor skills necessary to produce

TABLE 7
Frequencies by Which Different Kinds of Plants Used Specific Government Assistance (*Fortune 500* firms)

	Mover Plants	Newly Opened Plants
Industrial Revenue Bonds	17%	26%
Tax Concessions of Any Sort	28%	14%
Roads, Sewers, Water	3%	38%
Labor Training	6%	30%
Help With Environmental Permits	6%	22%
Zoning Changes	8%	12%
Expansion of Sewage Treatment	0%	10%
Traffic, Parking Adjustment	3%	6%

Source: Roger Schmenner. *Making Business Location Decisions* (Englewood Cliffs, NJ: Prentice-Hall, Inc.), 1982, p. 55.

goods. This enables large firms to reduce labor costs.[42] It is also noteworthy that plants that employ higher skilled labor are much less likely to move great distances for fear of losing access to a qualified labor pool. Schmenner also finds that 80 to 90 percent of all mover plants relocated within 20 miles of their former site.[43] Even though the demand for sewer, water, and transportation facilities varies considerably according to industry, small firms have less specialized production needs and therefore less need for specialized infrastructure than large firms. Small firms, on the other hand, have more difficulty obtaining appropriate financing in the capital markets than large firms.

While the analyst must be careful in overplaying his limited hand as regards what policies work, Roger Schmenner's comprehensive study develops some evidence that infrastructure-related approaches can make a difference and may be among the most important factors that governments can directly effect:

> The survey findings suggest, then, that states and localities should concentrate on helping their manufacturers with the physical items which go into selecting a plant's location, constructing it, and starting it up. States and localities should stand ready to offer the interested manufacturer (i) speedy and accurate information about potential sites, (ii) help in securing necessary environmental or zoning permits, and (iii) timely help with the roads, sewerage, water, waste treatment, and labor training which can make a difference to the start-up of a new manufacturing facility.[44]

The lateness of any state and local government involvement in the majority of business location decisions suggests that the public sector should not place undue emphasis on the potential of speculative investments in infrastructure to stimulate economic development. State and local officials have little input into the business location decision process until the site selection process nears completion.[45] A survey of selected economic development professionals underscores the limited applicability of infrastructure assistance to promote economic development. These professionals emphasize the importance of infrastructure to economic development but state that the relationship between the two is indirect.[46] As appears to be the general case with location factors, infrastructure is a factor—though seldom a controlling one—in the business location decision. Amid the arsenal of potential incentives, its absence may be more crucial than its presence. That is, everything else being equal, the jurisdiction without an infrastructure-related assistance program may be disadvantaged when compared to one that does offer such inducements. By the same token, it appears unlikely that such a policy by itself will offset other impediments to development: "It is important to keep in mind that, while infrastructure is a necessary ingredient for economic development, it does not guarantee economic growth . . . infrastructure investment is only one part of the overall management and planning process."[47]

The considerable literature on the importance of various factors that enter into the decisions of firms about the location of facilities, demonstrates little unanimity regarding the relative importance of the factors. Each decision has its own uniqueness. But as one recent survey of studies have pointed out, the location decision is not an exercise in economic history, but rather is predicated on what those making the decision believe will occur in the future: "(T)he relevant factors are not those in effect when the location decision is made, but those expected to be in effect in the future."[48]

This quality, the sensitivity of the location decision to future conditions, presents a case for the significance of strategic planning in the infrastructure investment decision. Both the jurisdiction hoping to attract and the firm seeking to move are focused on the future. And, the government with a concrete and realistic plan for the location, cost, and financing of its public works—with an ability to respond quickly in their provision as locational opportunities present themselves—will hold one more card in the development game.

Future Considerations

In linking capital and operating budget decisions with economic development considerations, governments are required to forecast economic trends. Local governments adopting this approach will probably find it necessary to expand their sphere of reference regarding economic events in order to make informed judgments. Factors that traditionally have not played a major role in the choice of capital projects will be incorporated into the planning process.

Both structural economic changes and technological innovation influence business location decisions which, in turn, influence the demand for public works. As domestic corporations become multinational corporations, increased mobility enables firms to reduce their dependence on specific sites, even though labor factors exert a strong influence on location decisions. Before the wave of vertical, horizontal, and conglomerate mergers that gave multinationals preeminence in the world economy, corporate international mobility was not an important issue for economic development. Today, it may be the most important.

Technological change is radically altering the means by which work is accomplished. Likened by some to the Industrial Revolution of the 19th century, the development of electronic technology is quickly changing the design and location of the workplace. It is not difficult to imagine the home becoming an alternative worksite for some, given the rapid spread of remote computer terminals.[49] If such arrangements become feasible and commonplace, the demand for mass transit and highway facilities may decrease as the demand for telecommunications networks increases. Whether or not the above example is an accurate forecast of the future, the process of articulating and evaluating the impact that future changes may have on the demand for infrastructure is important to any thoughtful planning process.

Traditional notions of infrastructure planning have already expanded to include facilities for higher education and to attract high technology industry. The North Carolina Research Triangle is a successful example of applications of infrastructure and strategic budget planning at the state level over an extended period of time.[50] Having embarked on this venture in 1959, North Carolina at the time had no model of success on which to pattern its strategies. In contrast, cities now hurrying to develop high technology centers and industries have the successful examples not only of North Carolina's Research Triangle, but of California's "Silicon Valley," Boston's Highway 128 complex, and others to look to as successful precursors.

An essential part of the forecasting process is the identification of factors that are beyond the direct control of state and local governments. State and local governments are not complete masters of their own fates. But this does not imply that officials should approach capital planning or economic development with fatalism; rather, a realistic calculation of limits should promote effective use of resources in pursuit of the achievable, as opposed to their squandering on the unobtainable.

The postwar shifts in demography and the nature and location of economic activity mean that a resurgence in infrastructure investment will not follow old patterns and trends.[51] Furthermore, the accommodative as opposed to stimulative aspects of most infrastructure investment are such that much of it should proceed apace with—as opposed to speculating on—economic development, if it is to be productive and affordable.

Much of the preceding discussion has been hortatory: what ought to be the components of infrastructure's connection between today and tomorrow and the importance of combining fiscal and physical planning with a prudent strategy that fosters, if not guarantees, the economic wellbeing of the community. But in the world of public works, little progress will be made without public support. Welding together such support into bond offerings and budget items is the job of the political leader, and the politicians, prodded by the media, have shown increasing interest in the subject. November 1983 saw a large number of bond issues amounting to nearly $4 billion devoted to roads, water conservation, and bridges voted through at the polls. Highly visible and large statewide contests were successfully waged in New York, New Jersey, Rhode Island, and Maine.[52]

Not only may promoting infrastructure policies be good politics, but a perceived failure on the part of officials to address capital spending needs may bring defeat at the polls. As a footnote to the Mianus bridge collapse in Connecticut, which was cited in Chapter One, the defeat the following fall of the incumbent First Selectman of Greenwich was attributed to voter reaction to the traffic disruptions caused by the disaster: "Someone had to take the brunt of this"—and the local politician was the nearest person against whom the public could lash out.[53]

The popular support for spending more on capital goods—maintenance, repair, construction—will require either a reordering of spending priorities or a willingness to pay more taxes and charges. This requires convincing voters that the improvements are needed, that they indeed are building prosperity. And that message evidently is getting through. In speaking of ten bond issues successfully passed in Baltimore for a variety of projects ranging from sidewalk repairs to renovating the civic center, a public official said that the issues "represent the bread and butter of the city's improvement, not just the fancy desserts."[54]

Endnotes

[1]Pamela Plumb to John E. Petersen, May 5, 1983.

[2]*The New York Times*, August 11, 1983, "Transformer Fire Blacks Out Garment District; Shuts Streets and Big Stores"; *The New York Times*, August 25, 1983, "Water Main Break On East Side Stops Subway for Hours."

[3]Stanfield, pp. 2016–2021; Associate General Contractors of America, p. 1; Choate, "Wednesday," p. 1.

[4]Lewis, et al., p. 8.

[5]*U.S. News and World Report*, September 27, 1982, "To Rebuild America—$2.5 Trillion Job."

[6]John Stacha, "Criteria for Pipeline Replacement," *Journal of American Water Works Association*, May 1978, p. 256.

[7]Harry P. Hatry and George E. Peterson, *Maintaining Capital Facilities, Executive Report* (Washington, DC: The Urban Institute), 1983, p. 6.

[8]Harry P. Hatry, *Maintaining the Existing Infrastructure: Overview of Current Issues in Local Government Planning* (Washington, DC: U.S. Department of Housing and Urban Development, Office of Policy Development and Research), 1982, p. 17.

[9]Ibid., p. 18.

[10]Hatry, Millar, and Evans, p. 41.

[11]Hatry, p. 11.

[12]See Gurwitz and Kingsley.

[13]Ibid., p. 201.

[14]Hatry and Peterson, p. 8.

[15]Rhett D. Harrell, *Developing a Financial Management Information System for Local Governments: The Key Issues* (Washington, DC: Government Finance Research Center, Municipal Finance Officers Association), 1980, p. 5.

[16]John B. Olsen and Douglas C. Eadie, *The Game Plan: Governance With Foresight* (Washington, DC: Council of State Planning Agencies), 1982, p. 19.

[17]Ibid., pp. 51–54.

[18]Ibid., p. 67.

[19]See Edward A. Lehan, *Simplified Governmental Budgeting* (Chicago: Municipal Finance Officers Association), 1981.

[20]Lennox L. Moak and Albert M. Hillhouse, *Concepts and Practices in Local Government Finance* (Chicago: Municipal Finance Officers Association), 1975, p. 65.

[21]Lehan, p. 10.

[22]Olsen and Eadie, p. 47.

[23]Hatry, Millar, and Evans, Appendix B.

[24]Government Financial Research Center. "Urban Services Polity Facilities Annexation" *Resources in Review*. Vol. 5, no. 5, September 1983, p. 18.

[25]Choate, "Wednesday," pp. 8–10.

[26]Richard J. Moore and Michael A. Pagano, "Emerging Issues in Financing Basic Infrastructure," in *Mobilizing Capital: Program Innovation and the Changing Public/ Private Interface in Development Finance*, ed. Peter J. Bearse (New York: Elsevier Science Publishing Company), 1982, p. 432.

[27]Hatry, p. 50. Hatry states, "Local governments are frequently faced with the option of constructing a new interceptor sewer that requires a maximum of 25 percent local funds or funding sewer line replacement projects typically requiring 100 percent local financing."

[28]Moore and Pagano, p. 433.

[29]Lewis, et al., pp. 6–9.

[30]Choate, "Wednesday," p. 8.

[31]Legislation introduced includes House of Representatives bill H.R. 6591, 1983.

[32]Roger J. Vaughan, *The Urban Impacts of Federal Policies: Economic Development* (Santa Monica: The Rand Corporation), 1977, p. 132 (hereafter cited as *Development*).

[33]Ibid., p. 134.

[34]Olsen and Eadie, p. 83; Vaughan, *Development*, p. 22.

[35]Hatry, p. 50.

[36]Ibid., p. 11.

[37]Ibid., p. 20.

[38]Susan S. Jacobs and Michael Wasylenko, "Government Policy To Stimulate Economic Development: Enterprise Zones," *Resources in Review*, vol. 3, no. 3, March 1981, pp. 6–8.

[39]Kenneth Biederman, "Address to the Municipal Finance Officers Association 1983 Annual Conference."

[40]Robert W. Schmenner, *Making Business Location Decisions* (Englewood Cliffs, NJ: Prentice-Hall, Inc.), 1982, p. 55.

[41]See David L. Birch, *The Job Generation Process* (Cambridge, MA: MIT Program on Neighborhood and Regional Change), 1979.

[42]Schmenner, p. 116.

[43]Ibid, p. 110.

[44]Ibid., p. 58.

[45]Edward Humberger, *Business Location Decisions and Cities: An Information Bulletin of the Community and Economic Development Task Force of the Urban Consortium* (Washington, DC: Public Technology, Inc.), 1982, p. 25.

[46]Ibid., p. 52.

[47]Eugene Franchett to John E. Petersen, April 29, 1983.

[48]*State Polity Reports*, "The Business Location Decision," October 5, 1983, p. 7.

[49]*The New York Times*, August 25, 1983, "American Business Finds Ireland a Land of Green Pastures," and, *Forbes*, September 12, 1983, "A Job With A View," p. 147.

[50]Joint Economic Committee, *Location of High Technology Firms and Regional Economic Development* (Washington, DC: Joint Economic Committee), 1982, pp. 46–54.

[51]Kamensky, John. "Budgeting for State and Local Infrastructure: Developing A Strategy." Unpublished paper, April 1983, pp. 22–25.

[52]*The Bond Buyer*. "Voters Authorize 89% of Bond Issues" (November 10, 1983), p. 1.

[53]*New York Times*, "Official Ties Defeat to Bridge Collapse" (November 10, 1983), p. B2.

[54]*Wall Street Journal*, "Voters Across Nation to Decide Tomorrow on $4 Billion of Tax-Exempt Financing" (November 7, 1983), p. 45.

ANNOTATED BIBLIOGRAPHY

Advisory Commission on Intergovernmental Relations. *Changing Public Attitudes on Government and Taxes: A 1981 Commission Survey.* Washington, DC: Advisory Commission on Intergovernmental Relations, 1981. (41 pp)

A national survey of citizens' views toward government and taxes. The U.S. Advisory Commission on Intergovernmental Relations, 1111 20th Street, NW, Washington, DC 20575. (202) 653-5540.

Allardice, David R. "Small-Issue Industrial Revenue Bonds in the Seventh Federal Reserve District." *Economic Perspectives,* Winter 1982, pp. 12–22.

Examines the background and use of industrial revenue bond financing in Illinois, Indiana, Iowa, Michigan, and Wisconsin. Federal Reserve Bank of Chicago, Research Department, 230 S. LaSalle Street, Chicago, IL 60690. (312) 322-5322.

American Public Transit Association. *Transit Fact Book, 1981 Edition.* Washington, DC: American Public Transit Association, 1981. (80 pp)

Summary tables of operating and financial data for all U.S. transit systems—both publicly and privately owned. The American Public Transit Association, 1225 Connecticut Ave., NW, Suite 200, Washington, DC 20036. (202) 828-2800.

American Society of Planning Officials. *Local Capital Improvements and Development Management. Literature Synthesis* (1977, 125 pp); *Analysis and Case Studies* (1980, 236 pp); *Executive Summary* (1980, 14 pp) Washington, DC: U.S. Department of Housing and Urban Development.

The report of an extensive study of local government approaches to the use of the capital allocation process as a means of achieving development objectives. HUD USER, P.O. 280, Germantown, MD 20874. (301) 251-5154.

Aronson, Leanne and Shapiro, Carol. *The State's Role in Urban Economic Development: An Urban Government Perspective.* Washington, DC: Public Technology, Inc., 1980. (73 pp)

An Urban Consortium Information Bulletin reviewing, from the local government perspective, issues, problems, and approaches for dealing with urban economic development concerns. Public Technology, Inc., 1301 Pennsylvania Ave., NW, Washington, DC 20004. (202) 626-2486.

Associated General Contractors of America. *Our Fractured Framework: Why America Must Rebuild.* Washington, DC: Associated General Contractors of America, 1982. (33 pp)

Identifies $909 billion in capital infrastructure needs in 11 functional categories. Available from the Associated General Contractors of America, 1957 E Street, NW, Washington, DC 20006. (202) 393-2040.

Ballard, Frederic L., Jr. and Currier, Thomas S. *Industrial Development Financing*. New York: Practising Law Institute, 1981. (640 pp)

The annual coursebook updating legal information and regulations concerning industrial development bond anticipation notes, commercial paper, and other tax-exempt financing for industrial development. The Practising Law Institute, 810 Seventh Ave., New York, NY 10019. (212) 765-5700.

Barro, Stephen M. *The Urban Impacts of Federal Policies: Vol. 3, Fiscal Conditions*. Santa Monica: The Rand Corporation, 1978. (187 pp)

An examination of the determinants of urban fiscal conditions, the direct and indirect effects of federal policies on urban conditions, and of local fiscal response to federal policies. The Rand Corporation, Santa Monica, CA 90406. (213) 393-0411.

Bates, John C., Jr. and Doty, Robert W. *The Impact of 1982 Federal Legislation on Tax-Exempt Financing*. New York: Sorg Printing Co., 1982. (23 pp)

Recent federal tax law changes regarding tax-exempt securities generally and industrial development bonds in particular. Sorg Printing Co., 111 Eighth Ave., New York, NY 10011. (212) 741-6600.

Baumel, C. Phillip and Shornhorst, Elmo. "Local Rural Roads and Bridges: Current and Future Problems and Alternatives." Paper presented at the 61st Annual Meeting of the Transportation Research Board, January 1982.

Reviews the history and development of the rural transportation system in the U.S. and underscores the deterioration of roads and bridges that has been brought about by larger and heavier farm equipment, increasing amounts of grain moving over rural roads, increased coal production and hauling, larger school buses traveling longer distances, and rail abandonment. Request copies from Elmo Shornhorst, Box 66, Harlan, IA 51537. (712) 755-5954.

Bearse, Peter J., ed. *Mobilizing Capital: Program Innovation and the Changing Public/Private Interface In Development Finance*. New York: Elsevier Science Publishing Co., 1982. (478 pp)

A collection of papers, written by analysts and officials from all levels of government as well as the private sector, concerning the structural transformations that are emerging in the world's advanced economies. Distributed by Greenwood Press, 88 Post Road, West, Westport, CT 06881. (212) 226-3571.

Beck, Melinda et al. "The Decaying of America." *Newsweek*, August 2, 1982, pp. 12–18.

Examines America's road, bridge, sewer, and rail network, presents statistics, anecdotes, and photographs to back its claim that the infrastructure is near collapse, looks for solutions in the proposed New York Reconstructure Finance Corporation. *Newsweek*, 444 Madison Ave., New York, NY 10022. (212) 350-2000.

Bennett, James T. and DiLorenzo, Thomas J. "The Limitations Of Spending Limitation—State and Local Governments: Off-Budget Financing and the Illusion of Fiscal Fitness." *Economic Review*, December 1982. pp. 14–20.

Examines the implications of the statistics showing that "off-budget enterprises" have put more than half of all state debt beyond the direct control of voters. *Economic Review* is published by The Federal Reserve Bank of Atlanta, P.O. 1731, Atlanta, GA 30301. (404) 586-8788.

Birch, David L. *The Job Generation Process*. Cambridge, MA: MIT Program on Neighborhood and Regional Change, 1979. (22 pp)

A national survey of the job creation potential of small businesses and large corporations based on Dunn and Bradstreet data. The MIT Program on Neighborhood and Regional Change, Massachusetts Institute of Technology, 77 Massachusetts Ave., Cambridge, MA 02139. (617) 253-1000.

Boyle, M. Ross. *Report on Survey of Local Chambers of Commerce on their Economic Development Activities*. Washington, DC: McManis Associates, Inc., 1982. (44 pp)

How five hundred sixty organizations nationwide attract, retain, and expand economic development activity in their communities. Contact M. Ross Boyle, Senior Vice President, McManis Associates, Inc., 1201 Connecticut Ave., NW, Washington, DC 20036. (202) 466-7680.

Bradbury, Katharine L.; Downs, Anthony; and Small, Kenneth. *Urban Decline and the Future of America*. Washington, DC: The Brookings Institution, 1982. (309 pp)

Data from 121 U.S. cities support the authors' thesis that those cities already suffering urban decline will continue to lose jobs and population; the study also catalogs theories of why urban decline occurs. The Brookings Institution, 1775 Massachusetts Ave., NW, Washington, DC 20036. (202) 797-6258.

Brecher, Charles and Horton, Raymond D., eds. *Setting Municipal Priorities, 1981*. Totowa, NJ: Allanheld, Osmun & Co., 1980. (212 pp)

An analysis of the issues and choices facing New York City as it seeks balance between the local private sector and the local public sector. Includes a review of the capital budget priority-setting process. Allanheld, Osmun & Co., 81 Adams Drive, Totowa, NJ 07512. (201) 256-8600.

Bureau of Government Research and Service. *Financing Local Improvements by Special Assessment. Vol. I and Vol. II*. Eugene: University of Oregon, 1982. (Vol. I, 54 pp; Vol. II, 142 pp)

Although the focus is on policies and procedures in Oregon, many considerations and problems are common elsewhere. Available from Bureau of

Government Research and Service, P.O. Box 3177, Eugene, OR 97403. (503) 686-5232.

Bureau of Governmental Research and Service. *Infrastructure Needs and Resources of Selected State and Local Government Programs in Oregon.* Eugene: University of Oregon, 1983. (60 pp)

This report is one part of a national study sponsored by the Joint Economic Committee of Congress which analyzes Oregon state and local government infrastructure needs and the projected financial resources available to meet them to the year 2000. Bureau of Governmental Research and Service, University of Oregon, P.O. Box 3177, Eugene, OR 97403-0177. (503) 686-5232.

Burnside, Thomas J. "Tax Increment Financing: 'Rational Basis' or 'Revenue Shell Game?'," *Urban Law Annual*, Vol. 22. 1981. pp. 283–301.

Discussion of the advantages and disadvantages of tax increment financing extensively referencing state statutes. *Urban Law Annual*, The Washington University School of Law, St. Louis, MO 63130. (314) 899-6478.

Business Week. "State and Local Government in Trouble." Special Report, October 26, 1981. pp. 135–181.

A comprehensive report on the fiscal problems of state and local governments. Published by McGraw-Hill, Inc., 1221 Avenue of the Americas, New York, NY 10020. Reprint Department: (609) 448-1700 x5550.

Chemical Bank. *Guide to State Capital Formation Incentives and Innovations.* Washington, DC: National Governors' Association, 1983. (154 pp)

A state-by-state review of development and financial incentives for economic development and capital formation. A single copy is available free, while supplies last, from the National Governors' Association, 444 North Capital Street, Washington, DC 20001. (202) 624-5300.

Choate, Pat. "House Wednesday Group Special Report on U.S. Economic Infrastructure." Washington, DC: House Wednesday Group, 1982. (19 pp)

An overview of the decline in America's capital plant and recommendations for legislative action. Available from the House Wednesday Group, 386 HOB Annex #2, U.S. House of Representatives, Washington, DC 20515. (202) 226-3236.

Choate, Pat and Walter, Susan. *America in Ruins: Beyond The Public Works Pork Barrel.* Washington, DC: Council of State Planning Agencies, 1981. (97 pp)

Documents the crisis state of the infrastructure of many of the nation's cities and proposes a national capital budget as a remedy. Available from Council of State Planning Agencies, 444 N. Capitol St., NW, Washington, DC 20001. (202) 624-5386.

Choate, Pat and Walter, Susan. "Public Facilities: Key to Economic Revival," in *The AFL-CIO American Federalist*, August 1981. pp. 3–9.

A summary and follow-up to the authors' *America in Ruins* book. Contact the AFL-CIO, 815 16th St., NW, Washington, DC 20006. (202) 637-5000.

Clinger, William F. "Testimony of Hon. William F. Clinger, Jr., before the Task Force on the Budget Process of the House Rules Committee" September 15, 1982. Washington, DC: mimeo, 1982. (5 pp)

Representative Clinger's statement on the need to include a capital budget in the federal budgeting process. Office of Representative William F. Clinger, Jr., 1221 HOB, U.S. House of Representatives, Washington, DC 20515. (202) 225-5121.

Coffin, Donald A. "Property Tax Abatement and Economic Development in Indianapolis." *Growth and Change*, Vol. 13, No. 2, April 1982. pp. 18–23.

An examination of the effectiveness of the Indianapolis tax abatement program that allows the establishment of redevelopment districts and the granting of a 10-year period of scaled property tax abatements within the districts. *Growth and Change* is published by the College of Business and Economics, University of Kentucky, 644 Maxwelton Court, Lexington, KY. (606) 258-8936.

Cole, Lisa A. and Brown, Hamilton. "Municipal Leasing: Opportunities and Precautions for Governments." *Resources in Review*, January 1982. pp. 6–9.

An overview of the kinds of leasing arrangements utilized by municipalities, including safe harbor leasing, with a discussion of the merits and pitfalls of municipal leasing. Published by the Government Finance Research Center, 1750 K Street, NW, Suite 200, Washington, DC 20006. (202) 466-2014.

Cole, Lisa A.; Duven, Dawn R.; Owen, Samuel H., Jr.; Vogt, A. John. *Guide to Municipal Leasing*. Chicago: Municipal Finance Officers Association, 1983. (239 pp)

A practitioner-oriented guide to lease-purchase and other leasing arrangements as a means for providing capital facilities. Municipal Finance Officers Association, 180 North Michigan Ave., Chicago, IL 60601. (312) 977-9700.

Committee on the Budget. *Tax Expenditures: Relationships to Spending Programs and Background Material on Individual Provisions*. Washington, DC: U.S. Senate, 1982. (315 pp)

Tax expenditures are defined as revenue losses resulting from federal tax provisions that grant special tax relief designed to encourage certain kinds of behavior by taxpayers; provides a description of each tax expenditure, an estimate of the revenue loss associated with it, an analysis of its impact, and a selected bibliography. For sale by the Superintendent of Documents, U.S. Government Printing Office, Washington, DC 20402. (202) 783-3238.

Community Development Division. *Program Guidebook To Help Meet Community Credit Needs*. Washington, DC: Comptroller of the Currency, 1982. (102 pp)

Profiles of technical assistance and programs available to national banks for helping them to meet community credit needs, including economic development programs, small business development and rehabilitation loans. Community Development Division, Office of the Comptroller of the Currency, Washington, DC 20219. (202) 447-0934.

Comptroller General of the U.S. *Effective Planning and Budgeting Practices Can Help Arrest The Nation's Deteriorating Public Infrastructure*. Washington, DC: U.S. General Accounting Office, 1982. (60 pp)

Concludes that four elements—assessment, planning, selecting, and controlling—are necessary for public organizations to successfully manage their physical assets. U.S. General Accounting Office, Document Handling and Information Services Facility, P.O. Box 6015, Gaithersburg, MD 20760. (202) 275-6241.

Comptroller General of the U.S. *Federal Capital Budgeting: A Collection of Haphazard Practices*. Washington, DC: U.S. General Accounting Office, 1981. (139 pp)

Analysis of capital investment data and the planning and budgeting experiences of 24 public and private organizations; concludes that a policy-level approach to capital investment must be added to the federal government's decisionmaking. U.S. General Accounting Office, Document Handling and Information Services Facility, P.O. Box 6015, Gaithersburg, MD 20760. (202) 275-6241.

Congressional Budget Office. *Public Works Infrastructure: Policy Considerations for the 1980s*. Washington, DC: Congressional Budget Office, April 1983. (137 pp)

Reviews current federal infrastructure policy in light of infrastructure needs over the coming decade. Includes a detailed examination of highways, public transit, wastewater treatment, water resources, air traffic facilities, and municipal water systems. Superintendent of Documents, U.S. Government Printing Office, Washington, DC 20402. (202) 783-3238.

Conley, Gary N. "Tax Abatement." *CUED Information Service Report*, No. 19, June 1982. (11 pp)

Describes several uses of tax abatement in Ohio to promote inner city development; examines the merits and disadvantages of tax abatement from both the city's and the developer's perspectives. National Council for Urban Economic Development, 1730 K Street, NW, Suite 1009, Washington, DC 20006. (202) 223-4735.

Conlon, Joseph P. *The Third Study of General Manufacturing Business Climates of the Forty-Eight Contiguous States of America*. Chicago: Alexander Grant & Company/Conference of State Manufacturers' Association, 1982. (98 pp)

The relative attractiveness to manufacturers of the general business climates of the states is analyzed and ranked. Alexander Grant & Co., 39th Floor Prudential Plaza, Chicago, IL 60601. (312) 856-0001.

CONSAD Research Corporation. *A Study of Public Works Investments in the United States*. Washington, DC: U.S. Department of Commerce, 1980. (5 volumes)

Massive documentation and analysis; examination of the condition, expenditure patterns and financing mechanisms of public capital stock; a detailed account of financing mechanisms used to fund state and local public works investment. Superintendent of Documents, U.S. Government Printing Office, Washington, DC 20402. (202) 783-3238. Stock No. 003-001-00087-9.

Copeland, Claudia. *Infrastructure: Building and Rebuilding America's Capital Plant. Issue Brief IB82129*. Washington, DC: The Library of Congress, 1983. (19 pp)

Discusses problems that have led to the current focus on the nation's infrastructure, issues that will be debated as Congress addresses these problems, and emerging legislative initiatives. Library of Congress, Congressional Research Service, James Madison Building, Washington, DC 20540. (202) 287-5000.

Council of State Community Affairs Agencies. *Economic Development—The State's Perspectives*. Washington, DC: Council of State Community Affairs Agencies. 1981. (88 pp)

A report summarizing a series of conferences of state development officials; discussions of targeting and linking development resources. The Council of State Community Affairs, Hall of the States, 444 North Capitol Street, NW, Washington, DC 20001. (202) 393-6435.

Davidson, Jonathan M. "Tax Increment Financing as a Tool for Community Development." *University of Detroit Journal of Urban Law*, Vol. 56, No. 2, Winter 1979. pp. 405–444.

Examines legal and economic aspects of tax increment financing as a strategy for redevelopment and looks at TIF applications in three states: Minnesota, Wisconsin, and California. Publication offices: 651 E. Jefferson Avenue, Detroit, MI 48226. (313) 961-5444.

DeVoy, Robert and Wise, Harold. *The Capital Budget*. Washington, DC: Council of State Planning Agencies, 1979. (73 pp)

An examination of the process of capital budgeting with emphasis on the economic consequences of state capital expenditures and the use of local governments' capital budgets for state economic development purposes. Council of State Planning Agencies, 444 North Capitol Street, NW, Washington, DC 20001. (202) 624-5386.

Drucker, Peter F. *The Unseen Revolution: How Pension Fund Socialism Came to America.* New York: Harper and Row, 1976. (260 pp)

An analysis of investment policies and practices of the country's major pension funds. Harper and Row Publishers, 10 E. 53rd Street, New York, NY 10022. (212) 593-7000.

Edgar, Robert W. "Capital Budgeting: Taking Charge and Taking Control." Testimony of Hon. Robert W. Edgar, before the Task Force on Budget Reform of the House Committee on Rules. Washington, DC: mimeo, 1982. (16 pp)

Testimony on the need for undertaking a special analysis of capital budgeting and a national inventory and assessment of public facilities. Available from the Office of Representative Robert W. Edgar, 2442 RHOB, Washington, DC 20013. (202) 225-2011.

Evans, James H. and Millar, Annie P. *Report on Survey of Central Capital Investment Priority-Setting Procedures in 25 Municipalities.* Washington, DC: Urban Institute, 1982. (51 pp)

How central management in 25 cities determines priorities and selects among numerous capital project proposals. Available from the Urban Institute, 2100 M Street, NW, Washington, DC 20037. (202) 223-1950.

Federal Highway Administration. *Highway Statistics 1980.* Washington, DC: U.S. Department of Transportation, 1981. (167 pp)

Comprehensive data on highway user taxation, state highway finance, highway mileage, federal aid for highways, and highway finance data for municipalities: counties, townships, and other units of local government. From the Public Affairs Office, Federal Highway Administration, 400 Seventh Street, SW, Washington, DC 20590. (202) 426-0660.

Fischer, John. *Highway and Transit Infrastructure: Repair Status and Prospects.* Issue Brief IB82122. Washington, DC: The Library of Congress, 1983. (13 pp)

The condition of America's transportation, past and current trends in federal spending for highways and transit, and emerging legislative initiatives. Library of Congress, Congressional Research Service, James Madison Building, Washington, DC. (202) 287-5700.

Florida Advisory Council on Intergovernmental Relations. *Strategic Investment of the Florida Retirement System Trust Fund: An Examination of the Legal, Economic, and Programmatic Considerations.* Tallahassee: Florida ACIR, 1982. (41 pp)

A feasibility study of targeting the investments of Florida's state pension fund. Florida ACIR, Suite 400, Lewis State Bank Building, Tallahassee, FL 32304. (904) 488-9627.

Fosler, R. Scott and Berger, Renee A. *Public-Private Partnership in American Cities: Seven Case Studies.* Lexington, MA: Lexington Books, D.C. Heath and Co., 1982. (363 pp)

An in-depth analysis of successful public-private relationships in seven cities (Pittsburg, Baltimore, Chicago, Minneapolis, St. Paul, Dallas, Atlanta, and Portland, Oregon); the techniques and processes through which community resources can be brought to bear on urban needs, especially those concerned with economic development and downtown revitalization. Lexington Books, D.C. Heath and Company, 125 Spring Street, Lexington, MA 02173. (617) 862-6650.

Foster, Richard W. "Infrastructure: Picking Up the Pieces." *State Legislatures*, November/December, 1982. (3 pp)

A brief overview of several states' activities aimed at improving deteriorating infrastructure. Published by the National Conference of State Legislatures, 1125 Seventeenth Street, Suite 1500, Denver, CO 80202. (303) 292-6600.

Garfield Schwartz Associates. *Local Infrastructure Planning in Maryland.* Baltimore: Maryland Department of State Planning, 1982. (110 pp)

A study of the amount, type, and quality of information on local capital stock available to localities in Maryland. Maryland Department of State Planning, 301 W. Preston Street, Baltimore, MD 21201. (301) 383-7700.

Gold, Steven D. *How State Governments Can Assist Local Governments to Raise More Revenue.* Denver: National Conference of State Legislatures, 1982. (27 pp)

Outlines state activities to assist localities in expanding their tax bases and rates; includes easing restrictions on creative financing mechanisms and lowering barriers to investment of local funds and bond issuance. National Conference of State Legislatures, 1125 Seventeenth Street, Denver, CO 80202. (303) 623-6600.

Gold, Steven D. *State Fiscal Indicators.* Denver: National Conference of State Legislatures, 1982. (107 pp)

More than 50 indicators of the fiscal activity of state and local governments; includes comparative data on states' debt and spending for streets, highways, schools, hospitals. National Conference of State Legislatures, 1125 Seventeenth Street, NW, Suite 1500, Denver, CO 80202. (303) 623-6600.

Government Finance Research Center. *Alternative Investing by State and Local Pension Funds: Summary of Surveys.* Washington, DC: Government Finance Research Center, 1980. (72 pp)

The findings of three surveys on alternative investing practices by 98 state and local pension funds. Government Finance Research Center, 1750 K Street, NW, Suite 200, Washington, DC 20006. (202) 466-2014.

_____. *Financing Water Pollution Control: The State Role.* Washington, DC: U.S. Environmental Protection Agency, 1982. (47 pp)

Data and discussion about state grant, loan, and other assistance programs concerned with municipal wastewater treatment financing. Available from the Government Finance Research Center, 1750 K St., NW, Suite 200, Washington, DC 20006. (202) 466-2014.

_____. *Public Pension Investment Targeting: A Survey of Practices.* Washington, DC: Government Finance Research Center. forthcoming.

_____. *State Roles in Local Government Financial Management: Comparative Analysis.* Washington, DC: Government Finance Research Center, 1979. (59 pp)

An analysis of the ways states exercise oversight and regulation of numerous aspects of local government financial management. Government Finance Research Center, 1750 K Street, NW, Washington, DC 20006. (202) 466-2014.

Guenther, Robert, "Cities Getting Part of Profits for Giving Aid to Developers." *The Wall Street Journal*, September 29, 1982. p. 35.

Describes cases of cities' entrepreneurship in promoting redevelopment.

Gunyou, John M. *Public-Private Partnerships for Economic Development: A Reference Manual for Local Government.* Denver: Denver Regional Council of Governments, 1982. (170 pp)

A guide to the creation, development and operation of public-private partnerships, and strategies and techniques for development and redevelopment. Denver Regional Council of Governments, 2480 W. 26th Ave., Suite 200B, Denver, CO 80201. (303) 455-1000.

Guritz, Aaron S. and Kingsley, G. Robert. *The Cleveland Metropolitan Economy.* Santa Monica: The Rand Corporation, 1982. (240 pp)

A detailed framework for analyzing the strengths and weaknesses of individual industries within the Cleveland metropolitan economy is presented in this report. The Rand Corporation, Santa Monica, CA 90406. (213) 393-0411.

Hagman, Donald G. "Landowner-Developer Provision of Communal Goods Through Benefit-Based and Harm Avoidance Payments (BHAPS)." Part I and Part II. *Zoning and Planning Law Report*, March and April, 1982. pp. 17–24, and pp. 25–32, respectively.

The increasing use of "developer exactions," "impact fees" and special developer assessments; examines legal and constitutional questions, allocative efficiency, and distributional fairness of these methods of financing public infrastructure. Published by Clark Boardman Company, Ltd., 435 Hudson Street, New York, NY 10014. (212) 929-7500.

Harbit, Douglas A. "Tax Increment Financing." *National Council For Urban Economic Development Information Service Report*, No. 1, September 1975. (7 pp)

An introduction to tax increment financing methods with brief case studies. National Council For Urban Economic Development, 1730 K Street, NW, Washington, DC 20006. (202) 223-4735.

Harrell, Rhett D. *Developing a Financial Management Information System for Local Governments: The Key Issues*. Washington, DC: Government Finance Research Center/Municipal Finance Officers Association, 1980. (42 pp)

A summary of a symposium of practitioners exploring major issues to be addressed in selecting and implementing a financial management information system. Government Finance Research Center, 1750 K Stret, NW, Suite 200, Washington, DC 20006. (202) 466-2014.

Hartley, David E. "Special Benefit Financing in California." *Resources in Review*, September 1983. pp. 6–10.

A description and consideration of the advantages and disadvantages of a variety of special benefit financing arrangements adopted by California localities in the wake of Proposition 13. The Government Finance Research Center, 1750 K Street, NW, Suite 200, Washington, DC 20006. (202) 466-2014.

Hatry, Harry P. *Maintaining the Existing Infrastructure: Overview of Current Issues in Local Government Planning*. Washington, DC: U.S. Department of Housing and Urban Development, Office of Policy Development and Research, 1982. (76 pp)

Survey of current state-of-the-art practices for estimating infrastructure condition and for conducting replacement analysis of infrastructure options. Predominant practices in these areas are also discussed. Superintendent of Documents, U.S. Government Printing Office, Washington, DC 20402. (202) 783-3238.

Hatry, Harry P.; Millar, Annie P.; and Evans, James H. *Capital Investment Priority-Setting For Local Governments*. Washington, DC: The Urban Institute, 1982. (76 pp)

Technical and organizational issues concerning the annual capital budget process and the process for making selections for the governments' multi-year capital improvements program. The Urban Institute, 2100 M Street, NW, Washington, DC 20037. (202) 223-1950.

Hatry, Harry P. and Peterson, George E. *Maintaining Capital Facilities, Executive Report.* Washington, DC: The Urban Institute, 1983. (30 pp)

Report identifies maintenance options that local governments can implement to alleviate infrastructure problems, including issues relevant to capital and operating budgets. The Urban Institute, 2100 M Street, NW, Washington, DC 20037. (202) 223-1950.

Hatry, Harry P. and Steinthal, Bruce. *Working Paper: Selecting Capital Facility Maintenance Strategies.* Washington, DC: The Urban Institute, 1983. (127 pp)

Focuses on the process by which local governments select the type and amount of maintenance for their capital infrastructure. The Urban Institute, 2100 M Street, NW, Washington, DC 20037. (202) 223-1950.

Hovey, Harold A. and Field, Joanne T. *Indicators of Urban Condition.* Washington, DC: Government Finance Research Center, 1982. (234 pp)

Examines economic, demographic, and sociological data in this search for an urban indicators report format; includes comparisons among central city governments regarding infrastructure condition. Published by the Government Finance Research Center, 1750 K Street, NW, Suite 200, Washington, DC 20006. (202) 466-2014.

Huddleston, Jack R. "A Comparison of State Tax Increment Financing Laws." *State Government*, Vol. 55, No. 1, 1982. pp. 29–33.

Compares four aspects of tax increment financing (TIF) laws that were enacted by 14 states prior to 1980. Published by the Council of State Governments, P.O. Box 11910, Lexington, KY 40578. (606) 252-2291.

Humberger, Edward. *Business Location Decisions and Cities: An Information Bulletin of the Community and Economic Development Task Force of the Urban Consortium.* Washington, DC: Public Technology, Inc., 1982. (118 pp)

Reviews the process and factors of the business location decision; includes improvement of infrastructure among the strategies and tools suggested to local officials for attracting, retaining, and stimulating business investment. Public Technology, Inc., 1301 Pennsylvania Avenue, NY, Washington, DC 20004. (202) 626-2486.

Illinois Department of Commerce and Community Affairs. *Special Service Area Financing Handbook.* Springfield, IL: State of Illinois, 1982. (40 pp)

A handbook for local government officials explaining how to use special service areas for providing improvements and/or services to particular geographic areas. Illinois Department of Commerce and Community Affairs, 222 South College Street, Springfield, IL 62706. (217) 782-3892.

Jacobs, Susan S. and Wasylenko, Michael. *Government Policy to Stimulate Economic Development: Enterprise Zones.* Draft. Chicago: presented at "Financing State and Local Governments in the 1980s'' Conference, January 16–17, 1981. (32 pp)

Discusses goals of enterprise zone legislation, research concerning the ability of enterprise zones to influence industrial location choices, and suggestions for improving enterprise zones' prospects for success.

Joint Economic Committee. *Location of High Technology Firms and Regional Economic Development*. Washington, DC: Joint Economic Committee, June 1982. (69 pp)

An examination of the factors that influence the location decisions of high technology firms based on a survey of high technology companies. Superintendent of Documents, U.S. Government Printing Office, Washington, DC 20402. (202) 783-3238.

Jones, Benjamin. *Tax Increment Financing of Community Redevelopment*. Lexington, KY: Council of State Governments, 1977. (11 pp)

A brief discussion of how tax increment financing works and policy issues to be considered; includes a case study of the Wisconsin Tax Increment Act of 1975. The Council of State Governments, P.O. Box 11910, Iron Works Pike, Lexington, KY 40511. (606) 252-2291.

Katzman, Martin T. ''Measuring the Savings from State Municipal Bond Banking.'' *Governmental Finance*, Vol. 9, No. 1, March 1980. pp. 19–25.

Describes a method for measuring the benefits of participation in a municipal bond bank and identified specific cost reduction mechanisms. Published by the Municipal Finance Officers Association, 180 N. Michigan Avenue, Chicago, IL 60601. (312) 977-9700.

Kayne, Jay. *Economic Development—The States' Perspectives*. Washington, DC: Council of State Community Affairs Agencies, 1982. (88 pp)

A summary of discussions on the scope and potential of state development activities at eight regional roundtables conducted in 1980 which involved development officials from 40 states. Council of State Community Affairs Agencies, Hall of the States, 444 North Capitol Street, NW, Washington, DC 20001. (202) 393-6435.

Kieschnick, Michael. *Taxes and Growth: Business Incentives and Economic Development*. Washington, DC: Council of State Planning Agencies, 1981. (128 pp)

A review and critique of the uses and effectiveness of tax incentives as a public investment. Council of State Planning Agencies, Hall of the States, 444 North Capitol Street, NW, Washington, DC 20001. (202) 624-5386.

Kieschnick, Michael. *Venture Capital And Urban Development*. Washington, DC: The Council of State Planning Agencies, 1979. (59 pp)

Issues of capital sources and structures—as they relate to young, small firms—and implications for state development policies. Council of State Planning Agencies, 444 North Capitol St., NW, Washington, DC 20001. (202) 624-5386.

Kirlin, John J. and Kirlin, Anne M. *Public Choices-Private Resources: Financing Capital Infrastructure for California's Growth Through Public-Private Bargaining*. Sacramento: California Tax Foundation, 1982. (101 pp)

Describes and illustrates a wide range of public/private agreements used in California to finance infrastructure: among them are payments-in-lieu-of-taxes, charges upon later development, profit-sharing and private development of public property. Published by the California Tax Foundation, 9211 11th Street, Suite 903, Sacramento, CA 95814. (916) 441-0490.

Korbitz, William E., ed. *Urban Public Works Administration*. Washington, DC: International City Management Association, 1976. (563 pp)

A training and reference volume providing comprehensive, authoritative and managerially-oriented coverage of one of the most significant local government functions. International City Management Association, 1120 G Street, NW, Washington, DC 20005. (202) 626-4600.

LaFollette, Cameron. "Public Pension Funds Being Channeled Into Local Economic Development." *National Journal*, August 21, 1982.

A look at recent practices and thought concerning the use of state and municipal pension funds as sources of "alternative financing" of urban programs. Published weekly by The Government Research Corporation, 1730 M Street, NW, Washington, DC 20036. (202) 857-1400.

L. F. Rothschild, Unterberg, Towbin. *Toll Road Bonds: Is Continued Improvement Likely?* New York: L. F. Rothschild, Unterberg, Towbin, 1981. (55 pp)

A summary of the financial condition of each of 25 major turnpike and bridge authorities; notes the poor maintenance of the streets, highways and bridges of the nation and the decline in highway and bridge construction. L. F. Rothschild, Unterberg, Towbin, 55 Water Street, New York, NY 10041. (212) 425-3300.

Lawrence, David M. *Local Government's Role in Economic Development: Legal and Financial Aspects*. Chapel Hill: Institute of Government, The University of North Carolina at Chapel Hill, 1982. (28 pp)

The first volume of the *North Carolina Economic Development Papers*, a series that emphasizes the role of the state and local governments in promotion, financing, regulating, participating in, and being influenced by private business activity. Institute of Government. University of North Carolina at Chapel Hill, Chapel Hill, NC 27514. (919) 966-5381.

League of California Cities. *Financing Economic Development. Vol. VI in the Economic Development Series.* Sacramento: League of California Cities, 1982. (31 pp)

Outlines the provisions of direct incentives (loans, leases, grants, cost write-downs, interest subsidies, etc.), special assessment districts, and other financial resources in the state that can be utilized in the redevelopment process. Ten volumes in the series from the League of California Cities, 1400 K Street, Sacramento, CA. (916) 444-5790.

Ledebur, Larry C. and Rasmussen, David W. *State Development Incentives.* Washington, DC: The Urban Institute, 1983. (133 pp)

A compendium of state business incentives and their targeting by geographical area, industry, and firm characteristics; includes the dollar volume of program activity. The Urban Institute, 2100 M Street, NW, Washington, DC 20037. (202) 223-1950.

Lehan, Edward A. *Simplified Governmental Budgeting.* Chicago: Municipal Finance Officers Associations, 1981. (86 pp)

A detailed examination of budgetary theory, techniques applied by practitioners and the perspectives that program leaders, chief executives, legislators and citizens bring to the budget process. Municipal Finance Officers Association, 180 North Michigan Avenue, Chicago, IL 60601. (312) 977-9700.

Lewis, David, et al. *Public Works Infrastructure: Policy Considerations for the 1980s.* Washington, DC: Congressional Budget Office, 1983. (137 pp)

A study of the cost effectiveness of infrastructure investment, the role of federal policies and funding levels, and an assessment of how changes at the federal level could affect state and local governments and private-sector beneficiaries of infrastructure services. For sale by the Superintendent of documents, U.S. Government Printing Office, Washington, DC 20402. (202) 783-3238. Stock no. 052-070-05849-8.

Litvak, Lawrence. *Pension Funds & Economic Renewal.* Washington, DC: Council of State Planning Agencies, 1981. (185 pp)

Presents the conceptual issues that must be understood to prudently pursue development investing of pension funds and the nuts and bolts information required to successfully implement it. Council of State Planning Agencies, Hall of the States, 444 North Capitol Street, NW, Washington, DC 20001. (202) 624-5388.

Litvak, Lawrence and Daniels, Belden. *Innovations In Development Finance.* Washington, DC: Council of State Planning Agencies, 1979. (167 pp)

How state governments can use policies directed at capital markets to enhance state economic development; includes a review of options for financing public infrastructure. Council of State Planning Agencies, Hall of the States, 444 North Capitol Street, NW, Washington, DC 20001. (202) 624-5388.

McCarthy, Larry. "Benefit Assessments: A Born Again Revenue Raiser." *Cal-Tax Research Bulletin, Cal-Tax News,* June 15–30, 1981. pp. 3–10.

A review of the history of benefit assessments, their status under Proposition 13, and recent attempts in California to expand their use. Published by the California Taxpayers Association, 921 11th Street, Suite 800, Sacramento, CA 95814. (916) 441-0490.

MacDonald, Keith, ed. *Waterfront Development: A Reader.* Boston: Coalition of Northeast Municipalities, 1981. (280 pp)

A resource book of issue papers, case studies, newspaper and magazine articles concerned with the revitalization on waterfronts in Northeast cities. Coalition of Northeast Municipalities, 131 Tremont Street, Boston, MA 02111. (617) 542-5444.

Matz, Deborah and Petersen, John. *Trends in the Fiscal Condition of Cities 1980–1982.* Washington, DC: Joint Economic Committee of Congress, 1982. (57 pp)

The results of an annual survey of 300 cities, 1980 and 1981 actual and 1982 estimated data on revenues, expenditures, and debt by city size and objective of expenditure; illustrates trends in curtailed capital spending. Available from Publications, Joint Economic Committee of Congress, Room G 133, Dirksen Senate Office Building, Washington, DC 20510. (202) 224-5171.

Merkowitz, David. *The 1982 Users Guide to Government Resources for Economic Development.* Washington, DC: Northeast-Midwest Institute, January 1982. (152 pp)

A ready reference to the structure and requirements of federal government programs for economic development at the state, county, and local levels and examples of how they can be used. Northeast-Midwest Institute, Publications Office, P.O. Box 37209, Washington, DC 20013. (202) 225-1082.

Moak, Lennox L. and Hillhouse, Albert M. *Concepts and Practices in Local Government Finance.* Chicago: Municipal Finance Officers Association, 1975. (454 pp)

A general treatise on local government finance that discusses the budget process, revenue sources, the administration of governmental enterprises, treasury functions, debt policy, and accounting policy. Municipal Finance Officers Association, 180 North Michigan Avenue, Chicago, IL 60601. (312) 977-9700.

Moist, Kathleen. *Export Development: The Local Role. An Information Bulletin of the Community and Economic Development Task Force of the Urban Consortium*. Washington, DC: Public Technology, Inc., 1982. (35 pp)

Outlines possible strategies for local governments to pursue in order to enhance the relationship between economic development and export development. Public Technology, Inc., 1301 Pennsylvania Avenue, NW, Washington, DC 20004. (202) 626-2886.

Moore, Richard J. and Pagano, Michael A. "Emerging Issues in Financing Basic Infrastructure." In *Mobilizing Capital: Program Innovation and the Changing Public/Private Interface in Development Finance*, pp. 423–447. Edited by Peter J. Bearse. New York: Elsevier Science Publishing Company, 1982. (478 pp)

In-depth survey of maintenance, fiscal stress, and financing mechanisms in 9 cities. Discusses the effectiveness of various infrastructure financing techniques. Elsevier Science Publishing Company. 52 Vanderbilt Avenue, New York, NY 10017. (212) 867-9040.

Myers, Will S. *Regional Growth: Interstate Tax Competition. A Commission Report*. Washington, DC: U.S. Advisory Commission on Intergovernmental Relations, 1981. (77 pp)

Examines the issue of whether interstate tax competition has brought about significant differential growth and whether such competition adversely affects the economic health of states. U.S. Advisory Commission on Intergovernmental Relations, 1111 20th Street, NW, Suite 200, Washington, DC 20575. (202) 653-5536.

National Association of State Budget Officers and National Governors' Association. *Fiscal Survey of the States: 1983*. Washington, DC: National Governors' Association, 1983. (41 pp)

A tabulation of each states' year-end balance and actions taken during 1983 to balance budgets. National Governors' Association, Office of Research and Development, 444 North Capitol Street, Washington, DC 20001. (202) 624-5300.

National Council for Urban Economic Development. *Creative Use of Financial Incentives*. Washington, DC: National Council for Urban Economic Development, 1981. (48 pp)

A conference supplement outlining the topics and discussions of a CUED seminar on using Community Development Block Grants (CBDG) and Urban Development Action Grants (UDAG) to leverage investment, federal credit programs, and employment training incentives. CUED, 1730 K Street, NW, Washington, DC 20006. (202) 223-4735.

National Council on Urban Economic Development. *Investing in The Future of America's Cities: The Banker's Role*. Washington, DC: Comptroller of the Currency/Administrator of National Banks, 1980. (83 pp)

Six case studies of bank participation in development activities. Comptroller of the Currency, U.S. Department of the Treasury, Washington, DC 20219. (202) 447-1768.

National League of Cities. "Urban Infrastructure: Foundation for Growth." *City Economic Development Supplement to Nation's Cities Weekly.* September 20, 1982. (4 pp)

A collection of essays on the status of the urban capital plant and the need for planning, management, and financing strategies. Published by the National League of Cities, 1301 Pennsylvania Avenue, NW, Washington, DC 20004. (202) 626-3000.

National League of Cities/U.S. Conference of Mayors. *Capital Budgeting and Infrastructure in American Cities: An Initial Assessment.* Washington, DC: NLC/ USCM, 1983. (62 pp)

Results of a December 1982, survey of 809 cities concerning capital budgeting practices, the physical condition of capital facilities, and their ability to finance repair, rehabilitiation, and replacement of capital facilities. National League of Cities, 1301 Pennsylvania Avenue, NW, Washington, DC 20004.

Newman, Michael. "Tax Increment Financing for Development and Redevelopment." *Oregon Law Review,* Vol. 61, No. 1, 1982. pp. 123–144.

Issues relative to broadening the use of tax increment financing to pay for streets, sidewalks, parking garages, pedestrian plazas, and other public improvements. Published by the University of Oregon School of Law, Eugene, OR 97403. (503) 686-3844.

New Jersey State Legislature. *An Act Creating the New Jersey Infrastructure Bank: Assembly Bill No. 2061, Introduced October 18, 1982.* State of New Jersey, The General Assembly.

Establishes a bank to make loans to local governments for financing a wide range of capital facilities. The General Assembly of New Jersey, State House, Trenton, NJ 08625. (609) 292-5135.

New York State Housing Finance Agency. *Effects of Tax-Exempt Financing in the State of New York.* New York: Housing Finance Agency, 1982. (approx. 200 pages)

Study of the purposes and uses of tax-exempt financing by each of the New York public authorities. Contact: Publication Information, New York State Housing Finance Agency, 3 Park Avenue, New York, NY 10016. (212) 686-9700.

New York State Legislative Commission on Public-Private Cooperation. *Working Together for New York's Economy.* Albany: State of New York, 1983. (57 pp)

An examination of New York's tax, financial, and organizational incentives to economic growth. Legislative Commission on Public-Private Cooperation, P.O. Box 7039, Albany, NY 12225. (518) 455-2855.

Office of Infrastructure Renewal, Port Authority of New York and New Jersey. *A Summary of Financing Mechanisms for Public Infrastructure Projects.* New York: Port Authority of New York and New Jersey, 1982. (55 pp)

The report provides a general overview of traditional and creative mechanisms for financing public infrastructure capital projects. Available from the Office of Infrastructure Renewal, Port Authority of New York and New Jersey, 54 West, One World Trade Center, New York, NY 10048. (212) 466-4370.

Office of Management and Budget. *The Budget of the United States Government, 1983: Special Analysis H: Federal Aid to State and Local Governments.* Washington, DC: U.S. Government Printing Office, 1982. (27 pp)

A summary of federal assistance to state and local governments. Superintendent of Documents, U.S. Government Printing Office, Washington, DC 20402. (202) 783-3238.

Olsen, John B. and Eadie, Douglas C. *The Game Plan: Governance With Foresight.* Washington, DC: Council of State Planning Agencies, 1982. (176 pp)

An overview of the theory and practice of strategic planning that relates successful business experience to management requirements in government. Council of State Planning Agencies, 444 North Capitol Street, NW, Washington, DC 20001. (202) 624-5386.

Page, Clint. "$118 Billion by Year 2000 for Sewers." *Nation's Cities Weekly,* January 10, 1983, pp. 1.

Article on the budgetary implications for governments at all levels if the public sewer systems goals of the Clean Water Act are to be met. The National League of Cities, 1301 Pennsylvania Ave., NW. Washington, DC 20004. (202) 626-3000.

Pascal, Anthony and Gurwitz, Aaron. *Picking Winners: Industrial Strategies for Local Economic Development.* Santa Monica: The Rand Corporation, 1983. (46 pp)

Presents a methodology for analyzing metropolitan economic development, identifying promising industrial targets, and estimating the consequences of sectoral interventions. The Rand Corporation, Santa Monica, CA 90406. (213) 393-0411.

Petersen, John E. *An Analysis of the Impact of the All Savers Certificate Plan on the Municipal Securities Market.* Washington, DC: Government Finance Research Center, 1981. (25 pp)

Analysis of potential shifts in tax-exempt investment patterns and changes in tax-exempt interest rates due to the planned introduction of a new type of tax-exempt savings certificate to be marketed by savings and loan and other financial institutions. Government Finance Research Center, 1750 K Street, NW, Suite 200, Washington, DC 20006. (202) 466-2014.

_____. *Creative Capital Financing in the State and Local Sector: Causes, Characteristics, and Concerns.* Washington, DC: Government Finance Research Center, 1982. (32 pp)

An overview of the reasons for, the operation of, and implications of new creative financing techniques being employed by state and local governments. Available from the Government Finance Research Center, 1750 K Street, NW, Suite 200, Washington, DC 20006. (202) 466-2014.

_____. "Financial Roundup for State and Local Governments: Public Capital Crisis?" *Resources in Review*, July 1982. p. 5.

A commentary on the quarterly data reporting state and local government receipts, expenditure, debt, prices, and cost indices. Published by the Government Finance Research Center, 1750 K Street, NW, Suite 200, Washington, DC 20006. (202) 466-2014.

_____. "Has the Municipal Bond Market Undergone Fundamental Change?" Address delivered at the Annual Conference of the American Public Power Association, New Orleans, LA, May 24, 1982. (5 pp)

Analysis of trends in the municipal bond market during recent decades with emphasis on taxable and tax-exempt yields, the spread between the mix of institutional vs. "household" investors. The Government Finance Research Center, 1750 K Street, NW, Suite 200, Washington, DC 20006. (202) 466-2014.

_____. "The Outlook for State and Local Government Finance." Statement before the Joint Economic Committee of Congress, July 20, 1982. (23 pp)

An overview of trends in volume and yields in both long-term and short-term tax-exempt markets that identifies factors affecting the attractiveness of tax-exempt investing compared with taxable investment vehicles. Government Finance Research Center, 1750 K Street, NW, Suite 200, Washington, DC 20006. (202) 466-2014.

_____. *A Summary of State and Local Government Public Employee Retirement System Investment Practices and Policies.* (142 pp)

_____. *Alternative Investing by State and Local Pension Funds: Surveys of Current Practices.* (55 pp)

_____. *Alternative Investing by State and Local Pension Funds: Case Studies.* Washington, DC: Government Finance Research Center, 1980. (75 pp)

A detailed examination of how public pensions are invested, their investment performance, and the extent to which the funds are invested for "socially useful" purposes. Government Finance Research Center, 1750 K Street, NW, Suite 200, Washington, DC 20006. (202) 466-2014.

Petersen, John E.; Cole, Lisa A.; and Petrillo, Maria L. *Watching and Counting: A Survey of State Assistance to and Supervision of Local Debt and Financial Administration.* Chicago: Municipal Finance Officers Association, 1977. (72 pp)

Tabulates and discusses state involvement in many components of local government debt and financial administration. Municipal Finance Officers Association, 180 N. Michigan Avenue, Chicago, IL 60601. (312) 977-9700.

Petersen, John E. and Hough, Wesley C. *Creative Capital Finance for State and Local Government*. Chicago: Municipal Finance Officers Association, 1983. (256 pp)

A practical explanation of new financing techniques and an examination of the benefits, pitfalls, and policy considerations associated with their use by local governments. Municipal Finance Officers Association, 180 North Michigan Avenue, Chicago, IL 60601. (312) 977-9700.

Petersen, John E. and Deborah Matz. *Trends in the Fiscal Condition of Cities*. Washington, DC: Joint Economic Committee, U.S. Congress, 1982. (57 pp)

The 1982 report of an annual survey of 300 cities' current budgets and fiscal position. Superintendent of Documents, U.S. Government Printing Office, Washington, DC 20402 (202) 783-3238.

Petersen, John E. and Spain, Catherine L. *Alternative Investing of State and Local Pension Funds: Summary of Surveys*. Washington, DC: Government Finance Research Center, 1980. (59 pp)

Presents findings of three surveys on the alternative, or socially useful, investment practices of 98 state and local pension funds. Available from the Government Finance Research Center, 1750 K Street, NW, Suite 200, Washington, DC 20006. (202) 466-2104.

Petersen, John E. and Spain, Catherine L. "Public Employee Retirement System Investment Performance and Alternative Investment Objectives." *Governmental Finance*, June 1981. (6 pp)

Summarizes MFOA studies tracking investment practices of state and local government pension systems. Published quarterly by the Municipal Finance Officers Association, 180 North Michigan Avenue, Chicago, IL 60601. (312) 977-9700.

Peterson, George E., et al. *America's Urban Capital Stock. 6 vols.* Washington, DC: The Urban Institute, 1979–1981.

Studies that evaluate the condition of urban capital facilities in six major U.S. cities and consider the financial requirements for keeping them in working order. The Urban Institute, 2100 M Street, NW, Washington, DC 20037. (202) 223-1950.

Peterson, George E. *The Impact of Federal Fiscal Policies on Urban Economic Development*. Washington, DC: Public Technology, Inc., 1980. (40 pp)

An Urban Consortium Information Bulletin identifying and discussing issues of federal tax and spending policy relative to local economic development. Public Technology, Inc., 1301 Pennsylvania Avenue, NW, Washington, DC 20004. (202) 626-2486.

Public Securities Association. *Statistical Yearbook of Municipal Finance*. New York: Public Securities Association, 1981. (243 pp)

An annual reference document covering trends and transactions in the municipal bond market. Public Securities Association, One World Trade Center, New York, NY 10048. (212) 466-1900.

Real Estate Research Corporation. *Iowa's Community Development Incentives: An Evaluation. Excerpts from Final Report—Community Development Finance Study*. Chicago: Real Estate Research Corporation, 1980. (36 pp)

The analysis, findings and recommendations of an evaluation of three community development programs in Iowa: tax increment financing (TIF), self-supported municipal improvement districts, and urban revitalization districts. Division of Municipal Affairs, Office for Planning and Programming, State of Iowa, 523 East 12th Street, Des Moines, IA 50319. (513) 281-3711.

Redfield, Kent and Brown, Dawn. *Special Districts in Illinois. vol. 1. Inventory of Special Districts: Powers & Numbers in Existence*. Springfield, IL: State Legislature, State of Illinois, 1979. (106 pp)

A catalog prepared for the legislature of information on special districts. Illinois State Library, Centennial Bldg., Springfield, IL 62756. (217) 782-5430.

Regional Planning Commission. *Catalog of Concepts on Capital Formation and Development Finance*. New Orleans: Regional Planning Commission, 1980. (153 pp)

A succinct description of approximately 50 concepts and programs throughout the nation that are concerned with capital formation and development finance. Regional Planning Commission, 333 St. Charles Avenue, New Orleans, LA 70130. (504) 568-6611.

Reinshuttle, Robert J. *Infrastructure: A Bibliography*. Lexington, KY: The Council of State Governments, 1983. (8 pp)

This report summarizes the major issues involved in the nation's infrastructure problem and follows with a corresponding bibliography of the literature available in each of these areas. The Council of State Governments, Iron Works Pike, P.O. Box 11910, Lexington, KY 40578. (606) 252-2291.

Reinshuttle, Robert J. *Economic Development: A Survey of State Activities*. Lexington, KY: The Council of State Governments, 1983. (47 pp)

Examines state economic development programs—state services offered to industry and local governments, promotional efforts, and state role in scientific research and development. The Council of State Governments, Iron Works Pike, P.O. Box 11910, Lexington, KY 40578. (606) 252-2291.

Research and Policy Committee. *Public-Private Partnership: An Opportunity for Urban Communities.* New York: Committee for Economic Development, 1982. (106 pp)

A Committee for Economic Development policy statement focusing on efforts to develop the local economy, neighborhoods, and community services. Committee for Economic Development, 477 Madison Avenue, New York, NY 10022. (212) 688-2063.

Resources in Review. "Sale-Leasebacks of Historic or Older Structures: An Alternative Capital Financing Option." Vol. 4, No. 5, September 1982. p. 2.

Outlines provisions of the Economic Recovery Tax Act of 1981 pertaining to sale-leasebacks for buildings more than 30 years old and explains how jurisdictions can enter into such arrangements. Government Finance Research Center, 1750 K St., NW, Washington, DC 20006. (202) 466-2014.

————. "Census Shows Special Districts on the Increase." Vol. 4, No. 5, September 1982. p. 11.

Gives statistics on local government units, including special districts, for the years 1962, 1972, and 1982 and outlines the kinds of special districts that exist. Government Finance Research Center, 1750 K St., NW, Washington, DC 20006. (202) 466-2014.

Rosenberg, Philip and Stallings, C. Wayne. *A Capital Improvement Programming Handbook for Small Cities and Other Governmental Units.* Chicago: Municipal Finance Officers Association, 1978. (76 pp)

A practitioner's desktop reference manual outlining the basic components of a sound capital improvement program and budget and providing step-by-step implementation guidelines. Publications Department, Municipal Finance Officers Association, 180 North Michigan Avenue, Chicago, IL 60601. (312) 977-9700.

Rudnitsky, Howard. "Tapping Pensions at Last." *Forbes*, December 20, 1982. pp. 58–60.

A report on recent pension fund purchasing of mortgage-backed pass-through securities being sold through the Federal National Mortgage Association. Forbes Inc., 60 Fifth Avenue, New York, NY 10011. (212) 620-2243.

Sacks, Seymour and Richter, Albert J. *Recent Trends in Federal and State Aid to Local Governments.* Washington, DC: U.S. Advisory Commission on Intergovernmental Relations, 1980. (95 pp)

Data and analysis of intergovernmental aids and their role in financing local government activities. The ACIR, 1111 20th Street, NW, Washington, DC 20575. (202) 653-5536.

Schmenner, Roger W. *Making Business Location Decisions.* Englewood Cliffs, NJ: Prentice-Hall, Inc., 1982. (268 pp)

An analysis of the motivation for and incidence of industrial location decisions, based on surveys of Fortune 500 companies, and firms in Cincinnati, Ohio and New England. Prentice-Hall, Inc., Englewood Cliffs, NJ 07632. (201) 592-2000.

Shannon, John., "Austerity Federalism—The State-Local Response." *National Tax Journal* XXXVI (September 1983): 377–382.

Historical trends in federal aid from 1954–1982. National Tax Association-Tax Institute of America, 21 East State Street, Columbus, OH 43215. (614) 224-8352.

Sharkansky, Ira. *Wither the State?* Chatham, NJ: Chatham House Publishers, Inc., 1979. (176 pp)

A thesis that much of the work of the state is being carried on "at the margins" by authorities, commissions, districts, and the like. Chatham House, Chatham, NJ 07928. (201) 635-2059.

Shubnell, Lawrence D. and Cobbs, William W. "Creative Capital Financing: A Primer for State and Local Governments." *Resources in Review*, Vol. 4, No. 3, May 1982. (4 pp)

An introduction to a number of nontraditional financing mechanisms available to municipal governments. Government Finance Research Center, 1750 K Street, NW, Suite 200, Washington, DC 20006. (202) 466-2014.

Simpson, Richard P. *California Public Employee Retirement: More Than a Gold Watch.* Sacramento: California Tax Foundation, May 1982. (68 pp)

Pension fund investment strategies and objectives, with emphasis on socially useful investing. California Tax Foundation, 921 11th Street, Suite 903, Sacramento, CA 95814. (916) 441-0490.

Stanfield, Rochelle L. "The Users May Have to Foot the Bill to Patch Crumbling Public Facilities." *The National Journal*, November 27, 1982. pp. 2016–2021.

The costs of repairing America's public works may have to be borne by the users of such facilities: a variety of user charge schemes are examined. Published weekly by the Government Research Corporation, 1730 M Street, NW, Washington, DC 20036. (202) 857-1400.

Steger, Wilbur A. and Dossani, Nazir G. *Public Works Investment (PWI): A Capital Budgeting Perspective.* Pittsburgh: CONSAD Research Corporation, 1982. (43 pp)

Congressional testimony on the need for a federal capital budget and a national inventory of public facilities. Available from CONSAD Research

Corporation, 121 North Highland Avenue, Pittsburgh, PA 15206. (412) 363-5500.

Stemmler, Hal, editor, "Financing—The Missing Tool." *Western City*, June 1982. (Entire issue)

The League of California Cities' special issue reporting redevelopment activities among the state's localities. California League of Cities, 1400 K Street, Sacramento, CA 95814. (916) 444-5790.

Stenberg, Carl and Warren, Charles R. *The States and Distressed Communities: The 1980 Annual Report.* Washington, DC: U.S. Advisory Commission on Intergovernmental Relations, 1981. (72 pp)

The initial report of a four-year analysis seeking to catalog and explain state efforts to aid distressed communities in five areas: (1) housing, (2) economic development, (3) community development, (4) fiscal reforms, and (5) local self-help programs. Advisory Commission on Intergovernmental Relations, Washington, DC 20575. (202) 653-5536.

Sternlieb, George and Listokin, David, eds. *New Tools for Economic Development: The Enterprise Zone, Development Bank and RFC.* Piscataway, NJ: Rutgers University, 1981. (231 pp)

Essays evaluating the potential of enterprise zones and a national development bank for revitalizing economically distressed areas. From the Center for Urban Policy Research, Rutgers Universtiy, P.O. Box 489, Piscataway, NJ 08854. (201) 932-3101.

Sullivan, Michael; Tropper, Peter; and Puryear, David. *Tax Incentives and Business Investment Patterns: A Survey of Urban and Regional Implications.* Washington, DC: Northeast-Midwest Institute, 1981. (61 pp)

Evaluates the urban and regional impacts of the numerous business tax incentives presented by the federal tax system. Northeast-Midwest Institute Publications Office, P.O. Box 37209, Washington, DC 20013. (202) 225-1082.

Task Force on Revenue Shortfall. *Revenue Shortfall: The Public Works Challenge of the 1980s.* Chicago: American Public Works Association, 1981. (111 pp)

The gap between available funds and public works needs: documented and analyzed from data based upon a sample survey of public works administrators from all the states. The American Public Works Association, 1313 East 60th Street, Chicago, IL 60637. (312) 947-2520.

Texas Municipal League. *Tax Increment Financing in Texas Cities.* Austin: Texas Municipal League, 1982. (143 pp)

A compilation of articles, laws and case studies describing how tax increment financing (TIF) is working in Texas since the passage of TIF legislation in 1977. Texas Municipal League, 1020 Southwest Tower, Austin, TX 78701. (512) 478-6601.

Triplett, Thomas J. *Investing in Minnesota: A Proposal to Use State Moneys for Maximum Benefit.* Minneapolis: The Minnesota Project, 1980.

An inquiry into the standards and goals that should guide the investment of state monies, the range of investment tools needed to achieve those goals, and policy recommendations for the State Board of Investment. The Minnesota Project, 618 East 22nd Street, Minneapolis, MN 55404. (612) 870-4700.

Tropper, Peter and Kaufman, Anne. *Pension Power for Economic Development.* Washington, DC: Northeast-Midwest Institute, 1980. (24 pp)

Discusses the potential for tapping the vast resources of the region's pension funds to undertake economic development and social investments. Northeast-Midwest Institute, P.O. Box 37209, Washington, DC 20013. (202) 225-1082.

Urban Institute/Winklevoss & Associates/Government Finance Research Center/Jump, Bernard, Jr. *The Future of State and Local Pensions. Final Report.* Washington, DC: U.S. Department of Housing and Urban Development, 1981. (approximately 300 pp)

A study of the major economic issues surrounding state and local pensions, including investment of pension plan assets. Distributed by HUD User, P.O. Box 280, Germantown, MD 20874. (301) 251-5154.

U.S. Conference of Mayors/National Community Development Association/Urban Land Institute. *Local Economic Development Tools and Techniques: A Guidebook for Local Government.* (83 pp);
————. *Economic Development: New Roles for City Government: A Guidebook for Local Government.* (60 pp);
————. *The Private Economic Development Process: A Guidebook for Local Government.* (33 pp). Washington, DC: U.S. Department of Housing and Urban Development/U.S. Department of Commerce, 1979.

Ways in which marketing, financing, zoning, taxing and other government actions can be enlisted for economic development objectives. Available from the U.S. Government Printing Office, Washington, DC 20402. (202) 783-3238.

U.S. General Accounting Office Staff. *Transportation: Evolving Issues for Analysis.* Washington, DC: U.S. General Accounting Office, 1982. (61 pp)

Focuses on major issues concerned with developing and maintaining an adequate and cost-effective national highway system and an intercity rail passenger service. Available from GAO, Document Handling and Information Services Facility, P.O. Box 6015, Gaithersburg, MD 20760. (202) 275-6241.

Vaughan, Roger J. *Rebuilding America, Vol. 1.* Washington, DC: The Council of State Planning Agencies, 1983. (234 pp)

A study of guidelines for financing infrastructure investments, including user fees, techniques employed in the tax-exempt bond market, and tax incentives. Council of State Planning Agencies, 400 North Capitol Street, NW, Washington, DC 20001. (202) 624-5386.

_____. *State Taxation and Economic Development.* Washington, DC: The Council of State Planning Agencies, 1979. (159 pp)

An exploration of what is and what should be the state's uses of tax policy for influencing economic development. Council of State Planning Agencies, 444 North Capitol Street, NW, Washington, DC 20001. (202) 624-5386.

_____. *The Urban Impacts of Federal Policies: Vol. 2, Economic Development.* Santa Monica: The Rand Corporation, 1977. (159 pp)

Discusses federal policies that directly influence economic development, distinguishing those policies affecting the level, growth, and distribution of demand from those affecting the price and availability of factors of production. The Rand Corporation, Santa Monica, CA 90406. (213) 393-0411.

Vaughan, Roger J.; Pascal, Anthony H.; and Vaiana, Mary E. *The Urban Impacts of Federal Policies, Vol. 1, Overview.* Santa Monica: The Rand Corporation, 1980. (20 pp)

The summary of a Rand Corporation research project evaluating the adequacy of existing knowledge as a basis for anticipating the effects of future federal decisions on urban areas. The Rand Corporation, Santa Monica, CA 90406. (213) 393-0411.

Vogt, A. John. *Capital Improvement Programming: A Handbook for Local Government Officials.* Chapel Hill: Institute of Government, University of North Carolina, 1977. (90 pp)

Describes a capital improvement program, outlines the steps involved in preparing a CIP, and shows how individual capital outlays are handled in the process. Institute of Government, University of North Carolina at Chapel Hill, P.O. Box 990, Chapel Hill, NC 27514. (919) 966-5381.

Walsh, Annmarie Hauck. *The Public's Business: The Politics and Practices of Government Corporations.* A Twentieth Century Fund Study. Cambridge, MA: The MIT Press/Twentieth Century Fund, 1980. (436 pp)

An analysis of the financing, administrative structure, and political functioning of state and local public authorities. MIT Press, 28 Carleton Street, Cambridge, MA 02142. (617) 253-2884.

Warren, Charles R. *The States and Urban Strategies: A Comparative Analysis.* Washington, DC: U.S. Department of Housing and Urban Development, 1980. (54 pp)

The overview and summary volume of a 12-volume series examining urban strategies in 10 states, U.S. Department of Housing and Urban Development,

Office of Policy Development and Research, Washington, DC 20410. (202) 755-4370.

Water Pollution Control Federation. *Sewer Charges for Wastewater Collection and Treatment—A Survey*. Washington, DC: Water Pollution Control Federation, 1982. (46 pp)

Contains a tabulation of sewer charge methods used by various municipalities and case histories of rate setting procedures followed in four communities. The Water Pollution Control Federation, 2626 Pennsylvania Avenue, NW, Washington, DC 20006. (202) 337-2500.

Watson, Rick. *Colorado and New York Evaluate Their Infrastructure Needs and Capital Budgeting Processes*. Denver: National Conference of State Legislatures, 1982. (30 pp)

A report of the existing financing methods and systems of capital budgeting underscoring the different problems faced by an older frostbelt state and a growing, sunbelt economy. National Conference of State Legislatures, 1125 17th Street, Suite 1500, Denver, CO 80202. (303) 292-6600.

_____. *How States Can Assist Local Governments with Debt Financing for Infrastructure*. Denver: National Conference of State Legislatures, 1982. (47 pp)

Evaluates eight techniques states use to assist local debt financing. National Conference of State Legislatures, 1125 17th Street, Suite 1500, Denver, CO 80202. (303) 292-6600.

_____. *State Aid For Local Capital Facilities*. Denver, CO: National Conference of State Legislatures, 1982. (88 pp)

Analyzes state capital grant programs to local governments for schools, sewerage, and transportation. National Conference of State Legislatures, 1125 17th Street, Suite 1500, Denver, CO 80202. (303) 292-6600.

Williams, Judith B. and Wise, Howard F., editors. *Main Street Ohio: Opportunities for Bringing People Back Downtown*. Columbus, OH: State of Ohio, 1981. (245 pp)

A comprehensive guidebook outlining methods for organizing and strategies for implementing commercial revitalization programs in Ohio. Ohio Department of Development, Office of Local Government Services, P.O. Box 1001, Columbus, OH 43216. (614) 466-2480.

Winters, Clint. "TIF: Revitalizing Texas Cities." *Fiscal Notes*, December 1982. pp. 6–12.

Texas officials' views of tax increment financing, ranging from a portrayal of TIF as a remedy to the problem of reduced federal funds to a rejection of it as a nightmare. State Comptroller, Office of Research and Statistics, P.O. Box 13528, Capital Station, Austin, TX 78711. (512) 475-1914.

Zimmerman, Joseph F. *Measuring Local Discretionary Authority.* Washington, DC: U.S. Advisory Commission on Intergovernmental Relations, 1981. (77 pp)

Research categorizing the components of local authority and developing an index to facilitate comparisons of local autonomy across jurisdictions. ACIR, 1111 20th Street, NW, Washington, DC 20575. (202) 653-5536.

GLOSSARY

ACCELERATED COST RECOVERY SYSTEM (ACRS)

The system of depreciation established by the Economic Recovery Tax Act of 1981 (ERTA) as amended by the Tax Equity and Fiscal Responsibility Act of 1982 (TEFRA). ACRS permits depreciation of the capital costs of eligible property using accelerated schedules over predetermined periods that are shorter than prior law useful lives.

ACTIVITY

A specific and distinguishable unit of work or service performed.

AMORTIZATION

Gradual reduction, redemption, or liquidation of the balance of an account. Payment of an obligation or debt over time.

APPROPRIATION

An authorization made by the legislative body of a government which permits officials to incur obligations against and to make expenditures of governmental resources. Appropriations are usually made for fixed amounts and are typically granted for a one year period.

APPROPRIATION ORDINANCE

The official enactment by the legislative body establishing the legal authority for officials to obligate and expend resources.

ARBITRAGE

The gain which may be obtained by borrowing funds at a tax-exempt rate and investing these funds at taxable rates.

ASSETS

Property owned by a government which has monetary value.

BALANCE SHEET

A statement purporting to present the financial position of an entity by disclosing the value of its assets, liabilities, and equities as of a specified date.

BALLOON PAYMENT

A large extra payment that may be charged at the end of a loan or lease.

BASIS POINT

One one-hundredth of one percent (0.0001).

BEARER BOND

A security that does not identify its owner. The security is presumed to be owned by the person possessing it.

BOND

A written promise to pay a specified amount of money on a specified date in the future, typically with periodic interest payments. By convention, the original maturity of a bond exceeds one year, making it long-term debt.

BOND ANTICIPATION NOTE (BAN)

Short-term interest-bearing security issued in anticipation of a long-term bond issuance at a later date.

BOND COUNSEL

An attorney (or firm of attorneys) retained by the issuer to give a legal opinion that the issuer is authorized to issue proposed bonds, the issuer has met all legal requirements necessary for issuance, and interest on the proposed bonds will be exempt from federal income taxation and, where applicable, from state and local taxation.

BROKER

A person or company that arranges financial transactions for a fee.

BUDGET DOCUMENT

The official written statement prepared by the budget office and supporting staff which presents the proposed budget to the legislative body.

BUDGET (OPERATING)

A plan of financial operation embodying an estimate of proposed expenditures for a given period (typically a fiscal year) and the proposed means of financing them (revenue estimates). The term is also sometimes used to denote the officially approved expenditure ceilings under which a government and its departments operate.

CALL

An option to purchase an asset at a specified price at a date in the future.

CAPITAL

Wealth (money or property) owned or used in business by a person or corporation—the net worth of a business by which the assets exceed the liabilities. The face value of all the stock issued by a corporation.

CAPITAL ASSET OR PROPERTY

Asset or property that has a useful life that extends for more than one year. Capital assets are classified into land, buildings, improvements other than buildings, and equipment or furniture.

CAPITAL BUDGET

A plan of proposed capital expenditures and the means of financing them. The capital budget is usually enacted as part of the complete annual budget which includes both operating and capital outlays.

CAPITAL IMPROVEMENT PROGRAM (CIP)

A plan for capital expenditures to be incurred each year over a fixed period of several future years setting forth each capital project, identifying the expected beginning and ending date for each project, the amount to be expended in each year, and the method of financing those expenditures.

CAPITAL LEASE

A lease of a capital asset that is treated as a sale. For example, a lease-purchase agreement, in which provision is made for transfer of ownership of the property for a bargain price at the term of the lease.

CAPITAL MARKET
A place or system in which the requirements for capital of a business can be satisfied.

CAPITAL OUTLAYS
Expenditures for the acquisition of capital assets.

CAPITAL PROJECTS
Projects which purchase or construct capital assets. Typically a capital project encompasses a purchase of land and/or the construction of a building or facility.

CAPITAL STOCK
As used in this publication, the term refers in a general way to infrastructure or capital assets.

CERTIFICATE OF DEPOSIT
A negotiable or non-negotiable receipt for monies deposited in a bank or other financial institution for a specified period for a specified rate of interest.

CERTIFICATE OF PARTICIPATION LEASE
A lease that is "fractionalized" or divided into shares, represented by certificates of participation, that are assigned or marketed to investors.

COMMUNITY DEVELOPMENT BLOCK GRANT PROGRAM (CDBG)
A U.S. Government program that was established in 1974 to develop viable urban communities by providing decent housing and a suitable living environment, and by expanding economic opportunities principally for persons of low and moderate incomes.

COMPOUND COUPON BOND
A bond on which the interest accrues semiannually but is not paid until maturity.

COMPOUND INTEREST
Interest charged on both the principal amount that is borrowed or lent and on interest that has been earned but not paid. Compound interest can be calculated using the single payment compound amount formula.

CONTRACTING OUT
Provision of a service by a private-sector firm to a governmental unit, especially where the government had previously provided that service using its own employees.

CONVERTIBLE DEBT
A feature of certain bonds that allows them to be exchanged by the owner for another class of securities, in accordance with the terms of the issue.

COST ACCOUNTING
Accounting which assembles and records all costs incurred to carry out a particular activity or to deliver a particular service.

COUPON RATE
The interest rate specified on coupons attached to bonds.

DEBT

An obligation resulting from the borrowing of money or from the purchase over a period of time of goods or services. Legal definitions of state and local government debt vary from state to state and are determined by constitutional provisions, statutes, and court decisions.

DEBT LIMIT

A maximum amount of debt that may be legally incurred. A debt limit usually only applies to general obligation debt and is most often expressed as a percentage of the taxable value of property in a jurisdiction.

DEBT SERVICE

Payments of principal and interest to lenders or creditors on outstanding debt.

DEEP DISCOUNT BONDS

Bonds whose sale price is significantly below par value.

DEFAULT

Failure to pay principal, interest, or any obligation when due, or the violation of a covenant made in connection with the incurrence of debt or an obligation.

DEFICIT

(1) The excess of an entity's liabilities over its assets (See Fund Balance). (2) The excess of expenditures over revenues during a single accounting period.

DEFINED BENEFIT PLAN

A plan in which the benefits to which an employee is entitled can be calculated without knowledge of contributions (except when return of contributions is considered a benefit).

DEFINED CONTRIBUTION PLAN

A plan in which the employer's obligation is to make certain contributions, but in which benefit levels are not specified.

DEMAND OPTION

See put option.

DEPRECIATION

Charges against earnings to write off the cost, less salvage value, of an asset over its estimated useful life. It is a bookkeeping entry and does not represent any cash outlay, nor are any funds earmarked for that purpose.

DISCOUNT

The difference between a bond's par value and the price for which it is sold when the latter is less than par.

DISINVESTMENT

A diminution of capital stock caused by a failure to replace capital as it is consumed, deteriorates, or is otherwise disposed of.

DOUBLE-BARRELLED BOND

Tax-exempt bonds that are backed by a pledge of two or more sources of payment.

ECONOMIC ASSUMPTIONS

Assumptions about economic factors (e.g., return on investments, future salary increases and CPI changes) affecting pension funding.

ECONOMIC LIFE

The period over which property is used by one or more users, with normal repairs and maintenance, for the purpose for which it was intended, without limitation by any lease term.

EFFECTIVE INTEREST RATE

Interest rate stated on an annual basis which varies depending on the number of times that interest is compounded, earned, or calculated during the year. For example, if interest is compounded at 12 percent only once a year, the effective, as well as the nominal, interest rate is 12 percent. However, if interest is compounded at 1 percent per month, which is a 12 percent nominal rate, the effective interest rate is actually 12.7 percent.

ENTERPRISE FUND ACCOUNTING

Accounting used for government operations that are financed and operated in a manner similar to business enterprises, and for which preparation of an income statement is desirable.

EXPENDITURES

Where accounts are kept on the accrual or modified accrual basis of accounting, the cost of goods received or services rendered whether cash payments have been made or not. Where accounts are kept on a cash basis, expenditures are recognized only when the cash payments for the above purposes are made.

FIDUCIARY

One who controls funds to be used or invested for the benefit of another rather than himself or herself.

FINANCE LEASE

Lease that arises when the lessee negotiates a price with a manufacturer or vendor for purchase of property, arranges for a financial institution or leasing company to buy the property, and then executes an agreement to lease the property from the financial institution or leasing company.

FIXED INTEREST RATE

An interest rate that remains the same over the full term of an agreement, contract, or obligation.

FLEXIBLE-RATE NOTE

See floating-rate note.

FLOATING-RATE NOTES

Short-term debt instruments with interest rates adjusted every six months to reflect a six-month interbank offered rate. (Also flexible-rate note or floating-security rate)

FLOATING SECURITY RATE

See floating-rate note.

FULL FAITH AND CREDIT
A pledge of the general taxing power of a government to repay debt obligations (typically used in reference to bonds).

FUND
An independent fiscal and accounting entity with a self-balancing set of accounts recording cash and/or other resources together with all related liabilities, obligations, reserves, and equities which are segregated for the purpose of carrying on specific activities or attaining certain objectives.

FUND BALANCE
The excess of an entity's assets over its liabilities. A negative fund balance is sometimes called a deficit.

GENERAL OBLIGATION BONDS
When a government pledges its full faith and credit to the repayment of the bonds it issues, then those bonds are general obligation (GO) bonds. Sometimes the term is also used to refer to bonds which are to be repaid from taxes and other general revenue.

GENERAL OBLIGATION DEBT
Debt that is secured by a pledge of the general taxing power of the issuer. Also known as full faith and credit obligation.

GRANT
A contribution of assets (usually cash) by one governmental unit or other organization to another. Typically, these contributions are made to local governments from the state and federal governments. Grants are usually made for specified purposes.

INDUSTRIAL DEVELOPMENT BONDS
State and local government bonds issued to finance private projects that are usually only backed by revenues from the facility being financed (industrial revenue bond). They are almost always tax-exempt, but only because they satisfy numerous legal requirements regarding the size of issue, use of proceeds, and degree of private-sector involvement. For an explanation of exemptions and restrictions see section 103 (b) of the Internal Revenue Code. (Also called industrial revenue bonds.)

INDUSTRIAL REVENUE BONDS
See industrial development bonds.

INFRASTRUCTURE
The basic installations and facilities on which the continuance and growth of a community depends, such as roads, schools, power plants, transportation, and communication systems.

INSTALLMENT PAYMENT
Partial payment of a debt or liability. An installment contract calls for period performance and payments.

INSTITUTIONAL INVESTORS
Investors such as banks, insurance companies, trusts, and pension funds.

INTEREST
The price paid for the use of money, or the return on investment obtained from investing or lending money.

INTEREST RATE
Ratio of interest payable at the end of a period to the money lent or borrowed at the beginning of the period.

INVESTMENT
Securities and real estate purchased and held for the production of income in the form of interest, dividends, rentals, or base payments.

INVESTMENT INSTRUMENT
The specific type of security which a government purchases and holds.

INVESTMENT POOL
Investment funds of local governments which are pooled for centralized investment.

INVESTMENT TAX CREDIT (ITC)
Reduces the tax liability of persons or firms engaged in a trade or business by a portion of the investment that they make in qualifying depreciable property. The credit is generally either 6 percent or 10 percent of the investment in tangible personal property, depending on the class life of the property under ACRS. It is 25 percent of qualifying rehabilitation expenditures on certified historic structures, and 15 or 20 percent of qualifying rehabilitation expenditures on non-residential buildings that are at least 30 years old.

ISSUANCE COSTS
The costs incurred by the bond issuer incident to the planning and sale of securities. These costs include underwriter's spread, financial advisor and bond counsel fees, printing and advertising costs, rating agencies fees, and other expenses incurred in the marketing of an issue.

ISSUE OF BONDS
Bonds sold in one or more series authorized under the same resolution or indenture.

ISSUER
A governmental unit or organization in whose name securities are issued or obligations incurred.

LEASE
An obligation wherein a lessee agrees to make payments to a lessor in exchange for the use of certain property. The term may refer to a capital lease or to an operating lease.

LEASE-PURCHASE AGREEMENT
A contractual agreement that is called a lease but that in substance is a sale. Also called a conditional sale, a conditional-sales lease, or an installment-purchase. If the lessee in such a transaction is a state or local government or other tax-exempt organization, the lease-purchase agreement can be a tax-exempt lease, meaning that the interest portions of the lessee's periodic payments are exempt from federal income taxes.

LEASE REVENUE DEBT
Debt that is secured by an obligation to make annual lease payments.

LETTER OF CREDIT
Bank credit facility wherein the bank agrees to lend a specified amount of funds for a limited term.

LEVERAGED LEASE
A lease involving at least three parties: a lessee, a lessor, and a lender. The lender provides substantial financing (leverage) to the lessor. In return, the lender has recourse to the property leased and to unremitted lease payments. A leveraged lease is a capital lease for accounting and financial reporting purposes and a true lease for federal income tax purposes. Leveraged leases are often used for large transactions in which multiple lessors and lenders are involved.

LEVERAGING
Magnifying the effect of economic development activity with an addition of funds from the private sector.

LIMITED LIABILITY BONDS
When a government issues bonds which do not pledge the full faith and credit of the jurisdiction, it issues limited liability bonds. Typically, pledges are made to dedicate one specific revenue source to repay these bonds, or some other special repayment arrangements are made.

LIMITED TAX BOND
A bond secured by a pledge of a tax or category of taxes which is limited as to rate or amount.

LINE ITEM BUDGET
A budget that lists the cost of items to be purchased.

LINE OF CREDIT
Bank credit facility wherein the bank agrees to lend, at its discretion, a pre-specified maximum amount of funds.

MARGINAL COST
The increase in the total cost of production that results from manufacturing one more unit output.

MATURITIES
The dates on which the principal or stated values of investments or debt obligations mature and may be reclaimed.

MORAL OBLIGATION BONDS
Bonds in respect to which a government, especially a state government, has asserted the intent of the legislative body to make appropriations sufficient to cure any deficiency in monies required to meet debt service for specified bonds but in respect to which the legislative body has no legally enforceable obligation to pay.

MUNICIPAL OBLIGATION
Generally, a bond, debt, or obligation issued or incurred by a state or local government.

NOMINAL INTEREST RATE

Interest rate stated as the same annual percentage regardless of the number of times interest is compounded, earned, or calculated during the year. For example, the nominal interest rate of 12 percent per annum remains 12 percent regardless of whether the interest is 12 percent compounded annually, 6 percent compounded semi-annually, 3 percent compounded quarterly, or 1 percent compounded monthly. See effective interest rate.

NOTE

A written promise to pay a specified amount of money at a specified date, with interest. By convention, the original maturity of a note is one year or less, making it short-term debt.

OBLIGATION

A duty imposed by law or contract; any written promise or contract to pay money or to do a certain thing.

OFFICIAL STATEMENT

A statement published by a government or another issuer at the time that it offers securities or other obligations for sale. The statement sets forth pertinent facts concerning the issuer, its financial conditions, the security pledged for the issue, and other facts deemed necessary for investors to judge the securities being offered.

OPERATING LEASE

A lease that enables the lessee to acquire the use of an asset only, not its ownership as in a capital lease. The lease term typically runs for only a portion of the asset's useful life.

ORIGINAL ISSUE DISCOUNT BONDS

Bonds which are sold at a substantial discount from their par value at the time of the original sale.

PENSION FUND

A fund established to provide for the payment of pension benefits.

PORTFOLIO

Holdings of securities by an individual or institution. A portfolio may contain bonds, preferred stocks and common stocks of enterprises of various types.

PREMIUM

Excess of the price at which a bond, security, or obligation is sold over its face or par value.

PRESENT VALUE

The equivalent value today of cash available at one time in the future or of a stream of payments in cash available at various times in the future. Present value varies with the level of the discount or interest factor applied to the future payment(s).

PRESENT VALUE METHOD

Analytic method that makes use of the single payment and/or the uniform series present worth formulas to convert one-time or annual or periodic costs in the future to their present value.

PRINCIPAL
The par value or face value of a bond, note, or other fixed amount security, excluding accrued interest.

PRIVATIZATION
A transfer to the private sector of activities and services usually or previously delivered by the public sector.

PRUDENT MAN RULE
An investment standard. In some states, the law requires that a fiduciary, such as a trustee, may invest the fund's money in a list of securities designated by the state. In other states, the trustee may invest in a security if it is one that would be bought by a prudent person of discretion and intelligence, who is seeking a reasonable income and preservation of capital.

PUT OPTION
The right to demand repayment of principal prior to a bond's maturity. In the case of short-term debt, this is referred to as a demand option.

REGISTERED SECURITY
Bond or security whose owner is identified on the bond or security and/or whose owner is registered with the issuer or its fiscal agent. Such a bond or security cannot be sold or exchanged without a change of registration.

RESERVE
An account used to indicate that a portion of fund equity is legally restricted for a specific purpose or not available for appropriation and subsequent spending.

REVENUE
The term designates an increase to a fund's assets which:
- does not increase a liability (e.g., proceeds from a loan);
- does not represent a repayment of an expenditure already made;
- does not represent a cancellation of certain liabilities; and,
- does not represent an increase in contributed capital.

REVENUE ANTICIPATION NOTES (RANs)
Notes issued in anticipation of the receipt of revenues, generally nontax revenues—especially revenues receivable from other governments.

REVENUE BOND
A security secured by the revenues of the operation being financed.

REVENUE DEBT
Bond, debt, or obligation for which principal and interest are payable exclusively from the earnings of a government enterprise. This term can refer more broadly to any state or local government debt that is not a general obligation debt.

REVENUE ESTIMATE
A formal estimate of how much revenue will be earned from a specific revenue source for some future period; typically, a future fiscal year.

REVOLVING LOAN FUNDS
Programs in which a specific amount of money is set aside to be used to make loans for a specific purpose. As loans are repaid, the money is re-lent, so there is a continuous turnover of the original assets.

SAFE HARBOR TRUE LEASE

Type of true lease authorized by the Economic Recovery Tax Act of 1981, which has since been restricted and will generally end for leases entered into after December 31, 1983. The "safe harbor" guarantees that a transaction will be characterized as a true lease for federal income tax purposes. Safe harbor true leases permit businesses without tax liabilities to sell and lease back depreciable property to businesses with tax liabilities. Such transactions are really sales of tax benefits rather than leases per se. The restrictions imposed by TEFRA on safe harbor true leases limit their profitability and have reduced their use. Governments are able to use safe harbor true leases only to lease mass commuting vehicles. The authorization for such commuting vehicle leases continues through 1987, and such leases are not subject to the TEFRA provisions that generally limit the tax profitability of safe harbor true leases. See the tax equity and fiscal responsibility act.

SALE-LEASEBACK

Arrangement in which an owner of property sells it to a financial institution or another buyer and simultaneously executes an agreement to lease the property back from the buyer. If such an arrangement is structured to be a conditional sale rather than a true lease, it is more properly called a sale-saleback rather than a sale-leaseback.

SECONDARY MARKET

The market in which bonds are sold at a time following their initial sale in the new issue market.

SECURITIES

Evidences of obligations to pay money or of rights to participate in earnings and other distributions of property. Staff to the SEC has held that participation interests in tax-exempt leases are municipal securities under U.S. securities laws.

SECURITY AGREEMENT

An agreement that creates or provides for a security interest. A creditor's security interest in personal property can be perfected by taking possession of the property or collateral for the property or by filing financing statements in the proper public records office.

SIMPLE INTEREST

Interest that is charged only on the principal amount borrowed or lent and not on interest that has been earned but not paid. Simple interest is calculated by multiplying the principal amount borrowed or lent by the interest rate per period, e.g., a year, by the number of periods for which the principal is outstanding.

SINKING FUND

A fund established in connection with a debt coming due on a fixed date which accumulates assets sufficient to pay the debt when it is due.

SMALL-ISSUE INDUSTRIAL DEVELOPMENT BONDS

Tax-exempt industrial development bonds, issued by government authorities as conduits to the private sector that are typically less than $10 million in size. Generally, the only backing for these bonds is the credit of the borrowing firm, the revenue from the projects financed, or the funded facility itself. There are maximum dollar, use, and other restrictions that must be met for these bonds to be tax-exempt. See section 103 (b) (6) of the Internal Revenue Code.

SPECIAL ASSESSMENT BONDS
A bond to be paid off from the proceeds of a special assessment.

SPECIAL ASSESSMENT DISTRICT
A legally established area for the express purpose of levying a special fee for public improvements that are of a special rather than general benefit.

STEPPED COUPON
A serial bond on which the coupon rate changes annually for all outstanding bonds rather than being uniform for all years for each bond of a given maturity.

TAX ANTICIPATION NOTES
Notes issued in anticipation of taxes which are retired usually from taxes collected.

TAX-EXEMPT COMMERCIAL PAPER
A very short-term security with maturity ranging from one to 270 days.

TAX-EXEMPT OBLIGATION
Bond, debt, or another obligation for which the interest paid is exempt from federal income taxes under Section 103 of the U.S. Internal Revenue Code or other federal legislation.

TAX-EXEMPT ORGANIZATION
An organization that may issue or incur tax-exempt obligations. State and local governments are tax-exempt organizations.

TAX RATE LIMIT
The maximum legal rate at which a municipality may levy a tax. The limit may apply to taxes raised for a particular purpose or for general purposes.

TERM
The period over which a bond, debt, or obligation is outstanding. Term usually refers to the full period between initial issuance and final maturity.

TREASURY BILL
A U.S. Government short-term security sold to the public each week, maturing in 91 to 182 days.

TRUE LEASE
A transaction that qualifies as a lease rather than as a purchase, installment-purchase, or conditional sale for federal income tax purposes. In a true lease, a lessee engaged in a trade or business can claim the lease payments as tax deductions, and a lessor in a trade or business can claim the tax benefits of ownership, e.g., depreciation.

TRUSTEE
A bank or trust company that holds title to or a security interest in leased property for the benefit of the lessee, lessor, and/or creditors of the lessor. A leveraged lease often has two trustees: one for the lessor(s) and an indenture trustee for the lender(s).

UNFUNDED LIABILITY
The difference between the assets and the asset target.
UNIT COST
The cost required to produce a specific product or unit of service (e.g., the cost to purify one thousand gallons of water).
UNDERWRITER
Generally, a person or firm that guarantees a price or a specific amount of financing for a transaction, e.g., a lease-purchase agreement. The term "underwriter" has varying and more precise meanings under specific federal and state laws.
URBAN DEVELOPMENT ACTION GRANTS (UDAG)
Large, general-purpose U.S. government grants that enable communities to undertake major projects that create a significant number of jobs.
USEFUL LIFE
Same as economic life, i.e., the period during which property is used by one or more users, with normal repairs and maintenance, for the purpose for which it is intended, without limitation by lease term.
USURY LAWS
Laws regarding the charging of interest rates.
VARIABLE INTEREST RATE
Interest rate charged under a lease or lease-purchase agreement that is subject to upward or downward adjustment during the lease term. A variable rate is typically pegged to a market index rate, e.g., the prime rate.
VARIABLE RATE BOND
A bond on which the interest rate is tied to other market rates of interest and is adjusted periodically.
VENTURE CAPITAL
Funds invested in enterprises that do not usually have access to conventional sources of capital.
WARRANT
(1) A certificate enabling the bearer to purchase additional bonds of a particular entity within a limited time-period at a pre-specified coupon rate.
(2) A short-term security that represents a liability of the issuer to be paid on a certain date, often placed directly with a vendor or a bank.
YIELD
The rate earned on an investment based on the price paid for the investment, the interest earned during the period held and the selling price or redemption value of the investment.
ZERO COUPON
A bond without current interest coupons sold at a substantial discount from par that provides its return to investors through accretion in value at maturity.